T0327838

SEASONS
OF THE
ZODIAC

SEASONS
OF THE
ZODIAC

**Love, Magick, and Manifestation
Throughout the Astrological Year**

STEPHANIE CAMPOS

FAIR WINDS

Quarto.com

© 2023 Quarto Publishing Group USA Inc.
Text © 2023 Stephanie Campos

First Published in 2023 by Fair Winds Press, an imprint of The Quarto Group,
100 Cummings Center, Suite 265-D, Beverly, MA 01915, USA.
T (978) 282-9590 F (978) 283-2742

Fair Winds Press titles are also available at discount for retail, wholesale, promotional, and bulk
purchase. For details, contact the Special Sales Manager by email at specialsales@quarto.com or
by mail at The Quarto Group, Attn: Special Sales Manager, 100 Cummings Center, Suite 265-D,
Beverly, MA 01915, USA.

27 26 25 24 23   1 2 3 4 5

ISBN: 978-0-7603-8489-3

Digital edition published in 2023
eISBN: 978-0-7603-8490-9

Library of Congress Cataloging-in-Publication Data is available

Design: Cindy Samargia Laun
Illustration: Caitlin Keegan

Printed in China

DEDICATION

For Melissa. I love you in every dimension and lifetime.

CONTENTS

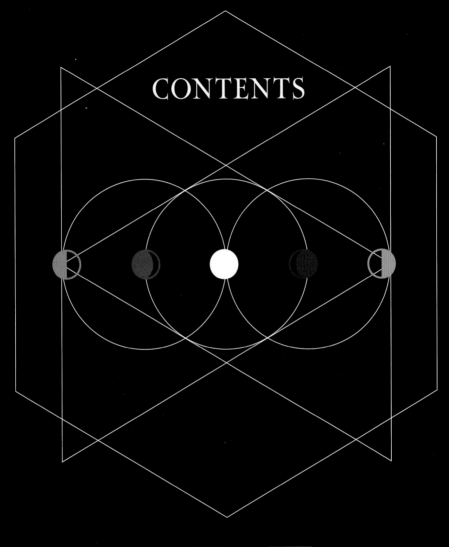

fire   earth   air   water

INTRODUCTION

The first time an astronaut travels in space, they sometimes experience a phenomenon called the Overview Effect. The Overview Effect is a cognitive shift—a transcendent experience that stems from witnessing your first glimpse of Earth floating in the limitless, uncharted territory of space. Those who experience it describe a sweeping range of emotions, in particular a feeling of being more interconnected with other humans and the Earth itself. It's a moment of transformation, leading to shifts in self-perception and value systems. For astrologers, who have been studying the stars and interpreting their messages for generations, this is no surprise.

Until someone agrees to send an astrologer to space (I'm ready when you are, NASA!), I can only begin to imagine how humbling this experience is. My own journey studying the stars has felt like a mini, personal version of the Overview Effect. Reflecting on the symbolism in my birth chart—a snapshot of all the planets' locations at the moment of birth—has brought solace, a greater capacity for self-compassion, and perspective, as well as a deeper sense of fate, destiny, and interconnectedness with life on Earth and the Universe itself.

Astrology is an art—not a science (although it was considered an academic tradition interwoven with the study of astronomy until the seventeenth century). As astrologers, we are messengers—translating the language of the planets and the stars and communicating those messages down to Earth. Each astrologer has a unique set of life experiences, privileges, and positionality and will, therefore, read the symbols differently. There is no one "right" way to interpret the cosmos, and we must approach this practice acknowledging and accepting these differences.

WHAT IS A ZODIAC SEASON?

Seasons of the Zodiac offers you a portal and permission slip to co-conspire with the Universe by accessing the different windows of opportunity that present themselves to us as the planets spin through the cosmos. A zodiac season is defined by roughly a thirty-day window when the sun is said to be "traveling through" a specific zodiac sign. This is also known as your sun sign in astrology. For example, if you were born during Taurus season, you're a Taurus. In Western astrology, which I practice and use as a foundation for this book, the zodiac sign seasons are no longer aligned with the constellations in the sky like they were thousands of years ago (although there is a system that does practice this called *sidereal astrology*). Instead, the zodiac seasons are based on fixed positions in the sky and align with the seasonal shifts we experience on Earth. For example, the start of Aries season always coincides with the Spring Equinox in the Northern Hemisphere. These zodiac seasons recur year after year in a pattern that forms the zodiac wheel, which is made up of all twelve zodiac signs. A full cycle takes 365.25 days to complete.

Each zodiac season carries different energetic signatures that are available for us to access. The zodiac season sections in this book offer general advice on different energies and themes that may present themselves during each seasonal shift. Each zodiac season will affect everyone differently based on their individual birth charts, but the insight provided in these sections can serve as a guide of what we might expect to unfold. These energies can help us identify what season of life we're in and how we can best use our resources. In other words, timing is truly everything. Aligning our intentions and desires with the natural ebbs and flows of planetary energy can help speed up our manifestations. We can pair our actions and intentions with the moon as it waxes and wanes in the sky, enhancing our opportunities for creating change, taking inspired action, and releasing what no longer serves us.

Now, to be clear, the zodiac seasons and planets don't "make" us do anything. We all have free will and can do anything we put our minds to, at any time. But for those of us who wish to live in connection with the cosmos around us, it is immensely helpful to know what sort of "vibes" are beaming down from above at any given time and how they may be mirroring our experiences, feelings, and behavior. In fact, it's not only helpful, it is transformational. Living in communion with the planets and witnessing their whispers, cycles, and patterns is humbling and awe-inspiring.

The information is this book should be used as a starting point. Each zodiac season differs year to year depending on where the planets are in the sky and the connections they are making with one another. Each season makes up one chapter in this book, and each chapter includes seven sections:

- An overview of the zodiac season itself
- Self-care tips to ground and center yourself during the zodiac season
- What to expect for your love life during each zodiac season
- Tips on how to use each zodiac season's energy to manifest
- Moon-based magickal practices, including each new moon and full moon per zodiac season
- A bespoke ritual based on every zodiac season
- Affirmations to use to tap into the zodiac season's energy

MOON MAGICK

While most of these sections are self-explanatory, to make the most of your lunar magick, it's helpful to understand a bit more about what new moons and full moons can be used for. Whether you're an established witch or simply dabbling in the mystical arts, once you hop on the highway to moon magick it's nearly impossible to go back. Using the natural lunar cycle as a guide to unlock your dreams is a surefire way to speed up your manifestation power and bring your desires Earth-side. Each zodiac season includes a minimum of one new moon and one full moon. Each lunation period carries a different energetic signature—new moons mark periods of new beginnings, planting seeds, and manifestation, while full moons signal a culmination point, release and, in some cases, an ending of sorts. Both the new moon and full moon can be used for manifestation work, and aligning our intentions and actions with these cycles can help us sync into a natural rhythm of surrendering and accepting change in our lives.

A FINAL NOTE

Before we begin, I want to make a final, important point. This book was written from my personal perspective—at the intersection of my own life experiences, unconscious biases, privilege, and positionality. Manifestation is a tricky topic because, yes, we all do have the ability to create the life of our dreams, but for many, especially people of the global majority, there are very real life circumstances, systems of oppression, and, of course, the degrading specter of white supremacy, embedded into the fabric of humanity that creates ongoing harm, obstacles, struggle, and challenges. It's also important to note that all of my personal astrological studies have been rooted in Western astrology, a lot of which, due to colonization, is rooted in the seasons and planetary alignments of the Northern Hemisphere.

It is my hope that this book helps you find more self-compassion and offers practical tools for you to access the magick of the Universe that surrounds us. May your dreams come true beyond even your wildest of imaginations—after all, we are all made of magick and stardust. Thank you for being here, I'm grateful for you and am sending you love in every single dimension.

Be brave enough to believe in your dreams.

When in doubt, ask your inner child for advice.

Lead with courage and confidence.

CHAPTER 1

ARIES SEASON

March 21–April 19

Grab your oversized shades and order an extra shot of espresso. As the first season of the zodiac, Aries season arrives with a bang, and once it's here, there's no playing catch-up. Aries season is the star of the show from approximately March 21 through April 19, coinciding with the Vernal Equinox. In the Northern Hemisphere, the Vernal Equinox marks the start of spring—when the Sun crosses the equator and starts traveling north. Aries season marks the astrological new year—when we begin our journey around the zodiac wheel once more. As the light of the Sun begins to take over the sky in the coming weeks, our energy, confidence, and zest for life increases, too. We're ready for a new adventure.

Throughout history, various cultures have celebrated this moment of sweeping change—from Ostara, a Druid and Wiccan tradition, to Passover, Nowruz, Shunbun no Hi, to Easter. In ancient Mesoamerica, the significance of the equinoxes were even woven into their architecture. The Chichén Itzá Temple of Kukulcan has feathered serpents at the base that are said to come alive during the equinoxes. At these times in the year, a shadow appears on the side of the temple staircase, creating an optical illusion of K'uk'ulkan, a serpent deity that the Maya worshiped. There is a deep well of traditions that align with and honor the timing of Aries season's arrival and its innate magick.

A time of new beginnings and fresh starts, Aries symbolism and magick are inherently tied to renewal, and the drive and determination to be an individual. To understand the essence of this season, first we must understand the qualities and core desires of Aries. As the first zodiac sign, Aries symbolizes the birthing process and our first breath. Ruled by the planet Mars, which is associated with the god of war, Aries enters the world after battling its way through the unknown and claiming its first achievement: the will to live and experience life full throttle. It's no secret that people born under Aries are born with an iron-clad backbone, confidence, and spirit that serves them well in any endeavor they decide to pursue. It's this boundless enthusiasm and inherent sense of curiosity and courage that defines the character of Aries season. Action-oriented Mars represents our drive, pursuit, anger, conflict, frustrations, sexual essence, motivation, and primal energies. Couple Mars' purpose-driven influence with the headstrong energy of the Ram (Aires' symbol), and it's no wonder that during Aries season we experience a resurgence of energy and newfound zest for life.

As we begin our journey through Aries season, we must first evaluate our relationship with ourselves. What are our needs and desires—and are they being met? In what ways have we sacrificed our passions or personal ambitions and wandered off our path? As the first fire sign in the zodiac, Aries represents the initial spark and first flame on Earth. It is during this season that we reignite our personal fire and feel into the hope and promise that with a little effort, confidence, and a refusal to back down, anything is possible. Every zodiac sign has specific qualities that it expresses. Aries is a cardinal sign, which is associated with the start of new seasons, leadership, and initiation. Aries season reminds us of our raw manifestation power. When we put action and effort toward our goals, the Universe receives this energy and meets us halfway. When we combine our will with action, we meet the wisdom of Aries season.

SELF-CARE TIPS FOR ARIES SEASON

Slow Down: Your mind is moving a mile a minute and you're full of inspiration—and eager to be the best, achieve the most, and do all of the above right now. Take time to consciously pause and be grateful for who you are, who you've been, and the journey that led you to this point in your life. Slow down for the sake of your soul—this creates space for introspection before jumping first into your next undertaking. You have no shortage of enthusiasm, so chose to move with intention and purpose.

Movement: Inviting more movement into your life is a wonderful way to tap into the energy of Aries season. If you have the privilege and ability, go on a daily walk to wake up your muscles and your physical being. Connect your physical movement with progress on your path and goals. Visualize walking toward a new destination or goal. Inspiration often strikes when we're on the move and taking in new scenery. If your movement is restricted or limited, a simple exercise of following your breath can work, too. Tune into the rising and sinking of your chest. As you exhale, let limiting beliefs exit your being. As you inhale, ask for inspiration and for Aries season to keep your passion burning bright.

Scream: It might sound dramatic, but an Aries season gift is reconnecting with our anger. In a society that often values our productivity over our well-being, we are rarely afforded the time to sit with our emotions and process them when they arise. What frustrations have you glossed over? When unaddressed, our feelings remain within our body and impact us. Practice a daily or weekly screaming exercise—while you're alone, in the shower, or into a pillow. Turn the volume up on one of your favorite songs and let residual feelings of anger, grief, and frustration leave your physical being.

YOUR LOVE LIFE + ARIES SEASON

Love at first sight is a universal Aries experience—this impetuous sign is quick to fall in and out of love. Aries season can bring anything from sudden, steamy flings that burn out quickly to a period of tending to the fires within our relationships and remembering the feeling of the initial spark that drew us to our loved ones. In Aries season, we're craving new experiences and adventures—whether single or partnered—and it's harder to keep our attention. We're feeling called to try new activities or travel to new places to keep the romantic embers burning. Aries season reminds us that life is meant to be *experienced* and that taking a risk, especially in matters of love, can lead to life-changing moments.

In Aries season, we want to be desired and be with the desirable. Tis the season to get dressed up and go out on date night! Tapping into your primal sexual energy and expressing it through the way you dress can take your relationship with pleasure to the next level. If you're single during Aries season, now is the time to pour love and energy into yourself. We must first fill our own cup before we can tend to another—it's self-love season! When you focus on activities and ambitions that truly feed your soul's essence, the Universe will conspire in your favor and recognize your alignment. Honoring every part of yourself—the good, the bad, and the ugly—will give you the confidence and magnetism you need when attracting an ideal partner or partners.

Couples should also think about tending to their individual desires during Aries season. If patterns of codependency have crept into your relationship, prioritizing solo time may be just what the cosmic doctor ordered. Taking time away from your partner and spending time on activities or hobbies that build your confidence and joy will only bring more harmony to your partnership. When you nurture your individual spirit, you can show up in your partnership replenished. Plus, you'll have new experiences to share at the end of your days. Focusing on your own passions and what ignites your inner flame may just remind your partner of why they were initially attracted to you.

HOW TO MANIFEST DURING ARIES SEASON: PLAY PRETEND

Remember when you were little and you used to play pretend? Maybe you'd dress up as a pop star and put on (in your mind) a full-blown, stadium-concert performance—complete with pyrotechnics and a giant, imaginary serpent adorning your neck. Your surroundings and the reality of the situation didn't matter; in that moment, you were the star you always dreamed of being. As the baby of the zodiac, Aries season magick is simple—it reminds you of the power of returning to your childhood wonder, beliefs, and curiosity. Don't be afraid to play pretend—try your future self on like an outfit. Embody that version of you now and pretend you are already there. How does your future version of yourself feel? How does your future version of yourself react to situations? Choose to embody your future self now.

We're impatient during Aries season, which can be a green light to push through any fears or discomfort, take action, and channel a new reality right now. Aries season is all about reconnecting with your inner confidence and letting it be your compass. Fake it until you make it! One of the best ways to do so is to use your imagination and visualization skills that came so naturally in childhood. If you choose to act like you've already achieved some of your desires, the Universe will recognize the signal you're giving off and send aligned manifestations accordingly. What are you waiting for? Embody your inner superstar now, and unlock the magick within this season.

TRY THIS!

Think back to the middle school or high school version of you. What hobbies or activities did you want to try but felt too shy or insecure to pursue? Well, throw away the imposer syndrome because it's time to invest in one of those pursuits. When you focus your energy on something that truly lights up your soul, your energy will be contagious. Focusing on your ability to cultivate more authentic pleasure in your own life will attract others to your infectious aura. Start with you!

ARIES SEASON **MOON MAGICK**

))) ◗ ● ● ● ◖ (((

Each Aries season includes a new moon in Aries and a full moon in Libra. The Aries-Libra axis brings our attention to our relationships—the ones we have with others and, just as importantly, the one we have with ourselves. The days these lunations take place will vary slightly from year to year. The following ideas can help you make the most of these portals.

New Moon in Aries

The new moon in Aries delivers a yearly lesson in destigmatizing the word *selfish*. We're reminded that when we align with our desires, turn inward, and prioritize what we hope to achieve during our time on Earth, we are living in alignment. The new moon in Aries reawakens parts of your identity that have been lying dormant. Where have you given your power away? In what ways are you ready to reinvent yourself? When you follow the unique urges of your soul, you are rewarded. The new moon in Aries asks you to show up fully, unapologetically take up space, and lead with confidence. It's time to upgrade your operating system and start acting like you know you will succeed. Your commitment to act will lead to a shift in your belief system.

The new moon in Aries is the first lunation of the astrological new year and has major New Year's resolution vibes. If you're ready to recommit to a goal or habit, call it in under this new moon. As a fire sign, we have that passion and drive to charge fearlessly after what we desire. If you knew that eventually you would succeed, how would that change the way you show up in the world? Let Aries season give you the courage to get out of your ruts and take a risk and try something new. Now is your time to remember who you really are, act accordingly, and step fully into your power. Over time, your effort will only lead to success. Ask yourself, *How would the future version of myself act or respond?* Be that version of you now. Your accomplishments are inevitable when you choose to believe you are worthy and deserving of what you desire.

Full Moon in Libra

The full moon in Libra signals a wake-up call within our partnerships and closest connections. Libra sits across the zodiac wheel from Aries, and it carries polar opposite qualities and concerns. If Aries is concerned with "me," Libra is focused on "we." There is inherent tension in all full moons—the Sun sits in one sign while the moon resides in the opposite zodiac sign. We're exploring our capacity for compromise and the balance in our connections. Do we too easily veer into the territory of people-pleasing and overextending ourselves? Or are we too self-centered? This full moon offers a cosmic review of our closest ties—whether that be platonic, romantic, or familial. The full moon in Libra asks us, "Are our relationships balanced?" If you've been putting in too much effort or too little effort, it's time to acknowledge this pattern and tip the scales.

This lunation also marks a period of climax—what did you manifest around the new moon in Libra last fall? The seeds you planted then are thriving now and we can see rewards and signs of our manifestations coming to life. This full moon tends to focus on matters of the heart. Perhaps we're ready to take the next step in a relationship or address any conversations that have been simmering and building tension. This is a turning point and a cosmic course correction for our relationships. If love isn't a top-of-mind priority during this season, this full moon can coincide with meaningful partnerships—work or friendships—showing up in your life.

TRY THIS!

If you want to use the full moon to manifest more love in your life, you can grab a rose quartz and meditate with it on Fridays, the day of the week that's ruled by Venus, the planet of love. Visualize the feeling you have when you're with your desired partner. Rather than getting caught up in the specifics of what they look like, focus on how they make you feel.

Burn Away Your Limiting Beliefs

Incorporating the element associated with each zodiac season into your magical practices can help you effortlessly tap into the energetic frequency of that zodiac sign. Since Aries is a fire sign, using a candle for your spellwork is a perfect conduit for Aries Season's magick. The color of the candle doesn't matter as much as you may think, so trust your intuition. White candles serve as blank slates, and red is associated with Aries and its ruling planet Mars; either would be a strong (but not required!) choice. This spell also calls for rosemary, which is associated with Aries and great for protection and cleansing, and lavender. Lavender carries a sense of calmness, which can temper our impulsive nature during this season.

- *Candle (recommended: white or red)*
- *Base oil (olive oil, coconut oil)*
- *Rosemary (3 stems)*
- *Lavender (2 stems)*
- *Pencil*
- *Paper*

1. Mix rosemary and lavender into your base oil to create a magickal oil to anoint your candle. Whisper a sweet intention or prayer over the oil while mixing to bless it with good energy.

2. Grab your piece of paper and pencil and write out a list of your fears and limiting beliefs.

3. Anoint the candle with your oil—rubbing it on the candle from the middle to the top, and then from the middle to the bottom, which signals a release of energy. When you're ready, burn your piece of paper with the flames of your candle. You can do this over a bowl of water for extra safety. As you watch your words dissolve into the flames, trust that you are now free from those fears.

4. Continue to let the candle burn until it goes out naturally and discard it, and any remains from your paper petition, in a garbage outside of your home.

ARIES
AFFIRMATIONS

My actions lead to my rewards.

I am courageous.

I am allowed to focus on myself.

I am worthy of my desires and dreams.

I am resilient.

My energy is contagious.

My passions will lead me to great heights.

I can start over whenever I choose to.

I am confident in my abilities.

I deserve to focus on myself. I am willing to take risks.

I am grateful for my failures.

My only competition is myself.

I love, honor, and accept every part of myself.

I am whole on my own.

Prioritize your physical body and your five senses.

Trust in the process and take it slow.

Be present and reconnect with nature.

CHAPTER 2

TAURUS SEASON

April 20–May 20

Did someone say patience? Welcome to Taurus season—you made it through the nonstop, whirlwind of Aries season, but can you recognize the power that becomes available to you when you choose to slow down and soak up the present moment? Taurus season reminds us to enjoy the simple pleasures of life—a freshly squeezed lemon from a tree in your backyard, the warmth of a blanket freshly out of the dryer, or watching the sun's rays explode a variety of refracted hues across the horizon as it rises and sets. Taurus season takes over the skies roughly between April 20 until May 20 and marks the first emergence of the crops above the equator. At this time of year, we move on from the go-getting energy of Aries, and are now tasked with pausing, sustaining, and committing. Although we're starting to see signs of our metaphorical crops sprouting, we still have a way to go.

In the Northern Hemisphere, Taurus season coincides with the sustained increase of daylight, which ancient astrologers linked with the concepts of abundance, power, control, fertility, and even stubbornness. It's when the harvest shows its first signs of life and success. We're moving in the right direction and our work is paying off. The figurative little green sprouts of our desires have fought their way to the surface and are continuing to grow. We know what is working and what is worth investing our time and resources into. The cold days of winter are behind us, and now we can ease up a bit and focus on the present. As one of the most sensual signs in the zodiac, Taurus has an unmatched ability to be fully present and soak up life moment to moment. Taurus recognizes the benefit of being in tune with one's physical body, nature, and surroundings. In this season, it's time to explore your relationship with pleasure and indulgence and reconnect with your five senses. Are you experiencing life in the present, or watching it pass you by?

Embodiment practices help us tend to the relationship with our physical being. No matter how many dimensions you've traveled to or how much magick you've witnessed in your life, humans are physical beings, after all, having a fragile and tangible earthly experience. Taurus season reminds us of the magick that exists when we focus on our connection with our physical body. All our senses are heightened—so don't be surprised if you find yourself in a hedonistic tailspin. Lean into it! (Within reason, of course.) Taurus is ruled by Venus, a planet of love, indulgence, pleasure, and desire. By nature, it yearns to survey the different ways our senses intersect with pleasure. You can use Taurus season to reconsider your understanding of comfort and luxury. Lead with gratitude and appreciate the simple ways your life is abundant right now—whether that's having a full fridge or taking a candlelit hot bath. We must resist projecting ourselves into the past or future, and instead focus on the present and all the joy that surrounds us in the now.

Symbolized by the Bull, the energy of Taurus season is strong, steady, and unwavering. As a fixed sign in the zodiac, Taurus can be set in its ways—it's motto might be, if it's not broken, why fix it? During Taurus season, we develop a trusted, grounded approach and aren't afraid to roll our sleeves up and put in the necessary work to achieve our goals. We're channeling the Bull's immovable force of will and are more inspired to resist distractions and others' projections as we dutifully commit to our path. We know what truly brings us joy, and during Taurus season we aren't afraid to defend it and go after it with full force. Our taste and tenacity are our superpowers.

SELF-CARE TIPS FOR TAURUS SEASON

Go on a Hike: As an earth sign, it's no surprise that Taurus loves nature. The existing beauty in the flora, fauna, and landscape that surrounds us is both simplistic and mind-blowing. Changing your scenery can lead to shifts in perspective. As you observe the sun setting over a rolling, golden hill, the wind whispering through leaves, or the mystical reflective qualities that appear on the surface of bodies of water, come back to the present moment. Remember that we are on a giant rock, orbiting around in space. You are here now, and our existence is limitless. There is so much left unknown. Connecting with the natural world and leaning into your appreciation for your current place in the Universe can offer a game-changing reality check that brings you back down to Earth, literally and figuratively, and grounds you in the present.

Get Physical: Movement is key to maintaining your physical, mental, and spiritual wellness. Find some type of exercise or movement that brings you joy and with Taurus' steadfast dedication, commit to it a few times a week. When you tend to your body as a temple, other areas of your life begin to flourish, too.

Treat Yourself: A little indulgence goes a long way! You don't have to spend beyond your means to find a way to reward yourself. Whether that's with a restorative massage, a T-shirt you've been eyeing for a few months, a new perfume, nail polish shade, or a nostalgic home-cooked meal. When you invest in yourself in ways that activate your five senses, you are brought back into your body. Our ability to not only be in the present but to enjoy it and make the most of it, sends signals to the Universe that we are grateful for where we are and what we have. In return, the Universe conspires to send more blessings that match our current blissed-out vibration.

YOUR LOVE LIFE + TAURUS SEASON

Love hits differently during Taurus season. With Venus, the planet of love and adoration, as Taurus' ruling planet, it's no wonder that this is one of the most sensual, cuddly signs in the zodiac. In love, we're seeking comfort, stability, and someone we can rely on. The novelty of Aries season has worn off and we want something that will last. The idea of discussing the future and our five-year plans suddenly makes our hearts skip a beat. In this season, we are tending to our connections in the way we care for the land—with consistency and forethought.

Our senses are also heightened during Taurus season, and touch becomes a much sexier pastime. How can you liven things up in the bedroom by engaging all your senses? Physical contact and enjoying the raw and primal benefits of living in a body that can experience pleasure becomes a priority. It's time to explore what pleasure looks like for you—whether single or coupled up. What are your desires and turn-ons? Don't be afraid to name and sample them—it will help you build a more honest and solid foundation with your partner or partners. When you practice being vulnerable, you can establish new levels of trust and intimacy within some of your closest connections. In turn, the seeds of your relationship will begin to bloom in breathtaking and beautiful ways.

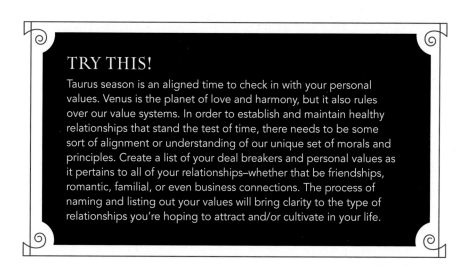

TRY THIS!

Taurus season is an aligned time to check in with your personal values. Venus is the planet of love and harmony, but it also rules over our value systems. In order to establish and maintain healthy relationships that stand the test of time, there needs to be some sort of alignment or understanding of our unique set of morals and principles. Create a list of your deal breakers and personal values as it pertains to all of your relationships–whether that be friendships, romantic, familial, or even business connections. The process of naming and listing out your values will bring clarity to the type of relationships you're hoping to attract and/or cultivate in your life.

HOW TO MANIFEST DURING TAURUS SEASON: EMBODIMENT

We're all guilty of rushing through our day with our to-do list looming in the background of our minds. When we pair our actions with intention, we free ourselves from some of the external pressure to be productive and can experience a greater sense of ease and flow. Whether we're walking, dancing, singing, or breathing, we can do so with purpose and pair it with an intention.

Embodiment, the art of giving physical form to a concept, idea, or energy, allows us to engage in a simple magical practice throughout our day. Pair your movement with something you hope to call in, increase, or manifest in your life. For example, let's say you want to work on your confidence. Set an intention that with every step you take that day, your confidence will increase. On your daily walk, visualize yourself walking toward a more confident version of you. Once you finish your walk, consciously choose to embody the confident version of you. How does it affect your attitude? Or the way you move through the rest of your day? With repetition, your subconscious will begin to operate with a more self-assured perspective.

TRY THIS!

Use your workouts to call in specific energies you wish to embody and bring into your life. For example, if you do a set of ten push-ups, pick one energy or desire you'd like to call into your life, like confidence or abundance. Each time you do a push-up, say that word either out loud or in your mind. As your muscles and body expand and contract, you'll associate the energetic frequency of that word or desire with your body's motion. In this process of embodiment, you will merge what your subconscious mind seeks with the physical realm.

TAURUS SEASON **MOON MAGICK**

)) ◗ ● ● ● ◖ ((

Each Taurus season includes a new moon in Taurus and a full moon in Scorpio. The Taurus-Scorpio axis in astrology brings our attention to matters related to new life and the closing of cycles, or death. The days these lunations take place shift each year. The following ideas can help you make the most of these magical moonbeams.

New Moon in Taurus

The new moon in Taurus asks us to check in with our pleasure, presence, and the physical world. How do you cultivate pleasure? When was the last time you lived in the moment? Do you actively make time for your desires? New moons deliver new beginnings, and in tactile Taurus, this lunation reminds us to shift our priorities and find some grounding. Our five senses are a gift, and we can cultivate relationships with them to sink deeper into the present moment. When you can recognize and appreciate the beauty and abundance around you through touch, taste, sight, sound, and scents, it becomes easier for more of that overflowing and supportive energy to find you.

This is also an aligned time to plant seeds related to a long-term goal that will require stamina and dedication. Where do you want to be six months from now? What projects require unwavering commitment? Set your intention and pick one action you can take now to make that a reality. You don't have to reach your goal within a week's time—slow and steady wins the race. Plow along confidently and at a comfortable pace like the Bull.

Comfort and security are also incredibly important to reflect on under a new moon in Taurus. What is your relationship with your resources? If you want to create a new financial goal or milestone, now's the time. What feeds your sense of security? In the meantime, rooting in the present and allowing yourself to unwind and relax will cultivate a deeper sense of trust. It sounds counterproductive, but Taurus knows the power that comes with surrendering to the now and taking breaks to relax.

Full Moon in Scorpio

One word: drama! What else would you expect from a full moon in temperamental Scorpio? With the moon in Scorpio, the Sun sits across the sky in the sign of Taurus, highlighting a very sensitive axis in astrology: life and death; what is comfortable and familiar vs. the taboo and the unknown, and consistency vs. transformation. The full moon in Scorpio also brings attention to our fears, trust, intimacy, and the ability to surrender. This lunation asks us to sit with emotions, feelings, thoughts, stories, and old versions of ourselves from the past that we've repressed or hidden. What is your relationship with shame and guilt? Full moons are a period of illuminating a topic and release. If we tap into Scorpio's deep well of emotional courage and confront some of the skeletons in our closet, we can be released from the past's grip on us and can experience a rebirth, too.

This full moon asks you to revisit your past and reflect on what parts of yourself you can forgive, send some compassion to, and release. When we surrender to any difficult feelings that arise and choose to move through them rather than avoid them, we can often experience a level of empowerment that we simply did not know existed. But first, we must engage in some shadow work. Shadow work involves dipping into your subconscious mind and reflecting on parts of your psyche that you repress or feel guilty or shameful about. We're choosing to hold a mirror to our shadow and instead of shaming that side of ourselves, embrace it. When we learn to love every corner of our inner being, we rise like a phoenix from the ashes. You can begin again whenever you choose.

TRY THIS!

Bring up a visual image of your shadow from a memory in your life when you felt shame, guilt, or stagnant. Imagine an energetic cord from your heart extending to their heart. Walk over and embrace your shadow. Feel into the cord's connection and know the warmth you're feeling is love and compassion pumping through the both of you. You are one and it's safe for you to accept every part of yourself.

Plant a Seed

We're bringing our focus to the earth element for this ritual. To witness our growth and dedication, we will pair one of our goals or desires with the planting of a seed. As you tend to it and witness its growth, be reminded of how far you've come.

- *Planter*
- *Soil*
- *Seed of your choice*
- *Water*
- *Intention*

1. Choose a seed that means something to you. Flowers are especially wonderful because they effortlessly tap into the Venusian beauty that Taurus adores. As you're preparing for this ritual, read up on the meaning and uses of the herb, flower, or plant that you're leaning toward and find any connection or correlation with what you are hoping to manifest and call in. What is it's role in its environment? What birds and bugs connect with it's life force and for what reasons?

2. As you plant the seed, focus on your desire, visualize it, feel into that future timeline, and once you've planted it, let it go. To enhance your desire, write down your intention and place it underneath the pot.

3. Over the next few months as you witness it's changing states, send gratitude and love into the seedling as you water and tend to it. Honor and recognize it's transformation and resilience as it overcomes the odds and fights to not only exist but thrive within the physical realm. This process will also water and nourish your goals and desires that you hope to bring Earth-side. It's an opportunity to witness the process of abundance over time and build slowly in true Taurus fashion. Try to time this exercise just after a new moon, as the moon expands and gains light. This is a season of growth and will feed our desires accordingly.

TAURUS
AFFIRMATIONS

I am grateful.

I am grounded.

I live in the present moment.

My sensuality is my superpower.

My desires are valid and worthy.

My dedication will lead to great rewards.

I am beautiful. I am valuable. I am worthy.

I deserve to focus on my needs.

When I nourish my body, I thrive.

My body is a sacred temple.

I invite in more spaciousness.

I listen to and respect my body's desires.

I choose to be embodied.

I am so grateful for the present moment.

I am constantly in a state of overflow.

The Universe is always conspiring to nourish and surprise me.

I trust that blessings are on their way to me.

Stay open and flexible—in both your mind and your plans.

Embrace a beginner's mindset.

Accept every part of yourself, especially the contradictions.

CHAPTER 3

GEMINI SEASON

May 21–June 21

Pay attention while you can—Gemini season brings a bevy of distractions, innovative ideas, and a lightening-speed pace. We rooted into our physical body during Taurus season and preserved our energy. Now, it's time to lighten the mood and project those energies outward. We're taking risks! We're saying yes to social engagements! We'll probably flake on a few people along the way, too. During Gemini season, which takes places roughly from May 21 through June 21, the energy is light, carefree, and curious. We're ready for a breath of fresh air.

This is a pivotal time in the zodiac, as we're entering a time of transition. In the Northern Hemisphere, we're approaching the longest day of the year: the Summer Solstice. This recognition arrives with a reality check: Our days will soon grow shorter and darkness will eventually take over the sky—so let's make the most of it! Adaptability and flexibility are associated with the zodiac sign represented by the Twins. As a mutable, or double-bodied sign, Gemini embraces the duality in all situations and is known for their varied interests. It's a busy season—from balancing your personal life and career, embracing your inner social butterfly and reigniting your love for your hobbies and passions—it's hard to slow down. You're being invited to fall in love again with every aspect of your life and every part of yourself. There's no need to sort through the contradictions there, you can simply allow all versions of yourself to coexist. They all serve a purpose.

During Gemini season, we begin to crave more variety, which all starts in the mind. Gemini loves to talk—we may be feeling chattier and more excited to share information or ideas. By engaging with others on a more intellectual level, we may also experience some shifts in our perspective, opinions, thought process, or the way we communicate. As the first air sign, Gemini is responsible for gathering facts and knowledge. In other words, we're curious little sponges during Gemini season! We approach life with more of an open mind. We become more welcoming of others' viewpoints. We're eager to expand our mind by trying new things, socializing with new people, or even engaging in more debates. Tending to our mental world is also an investment in our connections. When we have more to share, we feel like we're of value to our community. As we weave our new interests and wisdom into our daily conversations, we witness our own growth.

Ruled by Mercury, the planet of travel, communication, and the mind, Gemini season perfectly encapsulates that on-the-go energy, encouraging us to try out new social situations and push beyond our comfort zone. There is also a youthful and playful quality to Gemini season. We are interested in exploring new experiences and are able to lend ourselves grace as we readopt a beginner's mindset. We're not interested in being confined or living up to other people's expectations—our minds are pulled in multiple directions at once. And isn't that exciting? We're choosing to follow our curiosity.

Gemini's adaptability is an asset. It's during this season that we're reminded that changeability is a natural part of living on Earth. We are a work in progress. It's safe for us to evolve and change our mind. We are never fully in control. When we approach the unknown with an open and inquisitive attitude, blessings abound.

SELF-CARE TIPS FOR GEMINI SEASON

Practice Breathwork:	Every zodiac sign in astrology is associated with a body part, and one of Gemini's associations is with the lungs. Our breath is instinctive and necessary, yet it's often something that we take for granted and don't consciously acknowledge. Many of us are on autopilot. When we choose to intentionally focus on our breath, we can reduce anxiety and expand our mind's capacity. It also reminds us to be grateful for this simple but necessary bodily function. This is a wonderful practice to sort through the mental chatter and reestablish equilibrium.
Read a Book:	Give yourself a break from your to-do list and get lost in a book. Reading offers a little break from reality and can reduce stress all while improving your memory. As the traveler of the zodiac, Gemini knows that books can transport you to a whole other world—all while satiating your sudden thirst for knowledge and new experiences. Whether you're conscious of it or not, reading is a skill, and as you engage and work on it you're building self-esteem. Reading can activate your brain, igniting creativity within you.
Take a Class:	Your brain and body are craving new experiences during Gemini season. Have you always wanted to learn to play guitar? Perhaps you want to be fluent in another language? Or teach yourself some photo editing basics? Ruled by skilled Mercury, Gemini's wisdom lies in its ability to adapt and shapeshift. Pursuing a subject of interest and allowing yourself to adopt a beginner's mindset will stimulate both your body and brain in new and exciting ways. Over time, this will release a new well of creative inspiration as you test and strengthen your mental faculties.

YOUR LOVE LIFE + GEMINI SEASON

Who doesn't love witty banter? The quickest way to our hearts during Gemini season is through our mind. Communication, dialogue, and the exchange of information become the necessary cornerstones that nourish our connections. We're craving intellectual stimulation and connection—someone who will challenge us, hell, even debate with us! We want someone to fall in love with our minds—and someone we can learn from! What's the point of spending all your time with someone who has nothing new to add to your life? To lure in lovers during this season, we use our self-expression and put our variety of interests and knowledge on display.

During Taurus season, we established our sense of security, and now in Gemini season, it's time to test its durability. Are there any conversations you've been avoiding that may be creating cracks in an important relationship? This is a time to sink deeper into your self-expression and get honest with yourself and your partner. Express how you feel about one another and the future of your union.

Love during Gemini season can be peppered with words of affirmation and love poems galore—or it can bring up a tendency to overthink and use our words as weapons. Flirting comes naturally, and this is a time to explore your curiosity when it comes to love. Whether you're single or coupled, try something new—like a new restaurant, having sex in a new location in your house, or going out to a comedy show. Whatever you normally do, it's time to try the opposite! Gemini craves novelty, variety, and never shies away from taking a risk. When we lead with our curiosity and experience new events with a loved one, our bond strengthens. During Gemini season, you may find people harder to pin down; we're craving more freedom, so try not to take missed dates or cancelled plans personally.

TRY THIS!

Use the momentum of the season to have a check-in with your partner, roommate, or someone else you care about. Are your goals and values still aligned? Where do you hope to be in five years or five months? Gemini season helps us speak our mind, so use this space to clear any resentment or misunderstandings that may have built up over time.

HOW TO MANIFEST DURING GEMINI SEASON: THE WRITTEN WORD

"Spell" is in the word *spelling* for a reason. Words are spells—wield that power wisely! In astrology, Gemini is associated with the hands. It's ruled by Mercury, the planet of communication and writing, so learning to use written words as magical wands is one of this season's best-kept secrets. We're going old school for this manifestation tip, using our hands, paper, and a pencil as instruments. In the present tense, write out statements about who you want to be. What qualities does your future self have? If you have a specific goal in mind—what habits will it require of you to get there? Use phrases like "I am" instead of "I will"—we want to bring your manifestation to life through the present tense.

(continued on page 38)

Here are some writing prompts for you to explore and journal about:

- Write a letter from your future self to your current self. Describe your life in the future: What does your morning routine look like? What have you accomplished? Who do you socialize and share your energy with? What do you look like? How do you dress? What do you talk about or focus your mental energy on? Get specific about how you feel in this future timeline. Think about the experiences or hardships that you're experiencing now; what lessons has your future self learned from them?

- Write a list of your limiting beliefs. What nasty, cruel things do you say to yourself in the privacy of your own mind? Go through each item, one by one, and draw a big fat "X" over it. Reshape that belief or thought into a positive statement. For example, if one of your beliefs is "I'm not smart enough," cross it out and write something like, "My knowledge is always expanding and infinite."

- Write a letter to your teenage self—this time we're focusing on gratitude. Look how far you've come! Name and honor the insecurities and doubts that you felt then as you dreamed of accomplishing some of the goals that you are living with right now. Let teenage you in on all you've manifested and the moments of your life of which you're most proud of yourself.

TRY THIS!

Record the specifics of your future desires and affirmations in a voice memo. Listen to it before you drift off to sleep or before you get up for your day. During these semi-slumbering states, theta waves are present in our brain, which makes it easier to access our subconscious. Your brain is more easily influenced and can integrate your desires on an unconscious level.

)) ◗ ● ● ◖ ((

Each Gemini season includes a new moon in Gemini and a full moon in Sagittarius. Wisdom, sharing information, learning, and communication are of the highest concerns and priorities when the planets move through the Gemini-Sagittarius axis. The days these lunations take place shift from year to year. The following ideas can help you make the most of these moonbeams.

New Moon in Gemini

The effects of our yearly new moon in Gemini are felt first in the mind before they expand into the heart. This lunation brings a not-so-subtle shift in our thinking and perspective. With communicator Mercury as the ruling planet, our focus turns to how we self-express, what we believe, what knowledge we seek, and our friendships.

Gemini craves connection and this new moon is the perfect time to begin a new chapter regarding your social circle. It's a great time to start a course or commit to learning a new skill while connecting with a new community of people.

This is also a great moon for taking stock of our perspective. What are we spending our mental energy on? Think of it as your year in review in terms of what you've learned. Gemini energy is all about ideation, so some promising ideas for the future may also blossom under this lunation. What dreams and thoughts are you ready to express and bring to life in the real world? A new moon in Gemini can serve as a bridge and help make some of your whims and inspiration a reality. If you've been holding onto any feelings, this is also a powerful time to reconnect with your voice and self-express—particularly through the written word (break out your journal!). Sharing your thoughts and ideas under these moonbeams can lead to fertile rewards in the future.

Full Moon in Sagittarius

Information is on its way! If Gemini is about gathering information, Sagittarius is all about wisely disseminating it. A full moon in Sagittarius invites us to zoom out and focus on the big picture. The Gemini-Sagittarius axis is all about knowledge and wisdom. Gemini is concerned with collecting facts, its immediate environment, and all the details in front of them. Sagittarius is expansive and far-reaching with its Archer's bow and arrow (the Archer, half human and half centaur, is Sagittarius' symbol), ruled by overzealous Jupiter. During this lunation we're faced with holding the tension between our big-picture goals and the immediate steps we'll need to take to get there.

Full moons also magnify particular issues, themes, or concerns in our life, and this can signal the arrival of news we've been waiting for or a perspective shift. Information that arrives under this lunation can be inspiring and mark a culmination point where we learn news about some of our hopes and dreams materializing, but it's important to not bite off more than we can chew. Sagittarius has major go-big or go-home energy, and there can be a tendency to overcommit and overindulge.

TRY THIS!

As a visionary sign, Sagittarius reminds us that if we can believe it and see it, it's possible. Try a quick visualization. Close your eyes and imagine your end goal. Get detailed about your life in that reality. Now, imagine your soul floating above your body and continuing to move upward. As you rise into the sky, imagine your soul traveling backward on an illuminated path through time. Arrive at the present moment. Ask yourself: *What is the next step on my path?* The first words that come to your mind are informed by your intuition.

Divine Downloads

Journaling is the ultimate Gemini season practice to feel in sync with the cosmic energies, but automatic writing takes our potential to the next level. Automatic writing is a psychic exercise you can use to channel visions, thoughts, inspiration, and insight from your intuitive mind.

With consistent practice, this tool can help you effortlessly reveal the next stepping stone in your path as you access wisdom from your higher self.

- *Journal*
- *Pen*

(continued on page 42)

(continued from page 41)

1. Place a pencil and pen in front of you and begin by focusing on your breath. Feel your stomach expand and contract and follow your breath as it moves down your nasal passageway and fills up your lungs.

2. In your mind's eye, picture a whiteboard with random thoughts, worries, fears, doodles, and notes all over it. Now imagine your psychic eraser and wipe it blank, so you're now staring at an empty board.

3. Once you're able to focus on the empty board in front of you, pick up your pencil. Don't skip a beat—just begin to move your hand. Follow your hand's movements, keeping your mind blank. Let whatever comes up pour out of you—images, phrases, sentences, numbers, it doesn't matter. The key to getting started is to just start moving your hand and the words will follow. Pretend there is a magnet on the other side of your piece of paper, luring your hand toward it. You can even close your eyes as you scribe to keep focus on that blank board in front of you.

4. When you've finished, look at what is teleported onto your paper. A lot of it might feel like nonsense, but trust that there are kernels of wisdom to be mined there. Look for standout phrases or sentences. With repetition, this exercise supports and expands our creative faculties and activates our imagination. Unexpected wisdom can come through and also reinforce intuitive nudges we've felt but have talked ourselves out of exploring.

5. To further focus the exercise, you can set an intention at the beginning of the session like, "This session will reveal the next step to take in my business" or "This session will offer guidance on how to release my scarcity mindset." Just make sure that as you clear your metaphorical whiteboard you release the intention. You want your mind to be blank as you take pencil to paper.

GEMINI
AFFIRMATIONS

My curiosity is an asset.

I gain wisdom every time I try something new.

My failures lead to my successes.

I am adaptable.

I welcome change.

My perspective is always evolving.

My words are wands.

I am resourceful.

I am always willing to learn.

I speak my desires into existence.

I recognize the beauty in duality.

My mind is fertile, and I choose to always tend to it.

Socializing feeds my soul.

My next big idea is just around the corner.

It is safe for me to express myself.

I shape my reality with my words and thoughts.

Spend time with your chosen family.

Cultivate an environment that feeds your soul.

Love and care for others as a radical act.

CHAPTER 4

CANCER SEASON

June 21–July 22

Things are about to get a little more personal. Gemini season had us zipping from social event to social event and leaning into a more extroverted version of ourselves. By contrast, Cancer season, which begins near June 21 and ends around July 22, is a time to slow down and recalibrate. We're in a more introspective and reflective mood, and as we make space for our comforts and needs, we naturally have more time to consider our emotions.

Cancer season's arrival always coincides with the Summer Solstice, the longest day of the year. A cardinal sign that loves to initiate, it represents the sweeping change of seasons. We're leaving spring behind us and gearing up for some summer fun. In witch world, the Summer Solstice creates a portal into an otherworldly space—the connection between the physical world and spiritual realm is palpable on this day as the veil is thin. It serves as an energetic reset and cosmic check-in point but, most importantly, a moment of celebration. Going back centuries—or longer—cultures around the world have recognized the significance of the longest day of the year. It's a time to give appreciation for the Sun's warmth and bounty.

Cancer season is also a time of nesting and reconnecting to our roots. Ruled by the moon, which is associated with our memories, this season prompts us to reflect on our past and what home and family mean to us. We are contemplating our relationship with comfort, safety, and security. We want to cultivate a supportive and nurturing environment around us, as Cancer is incredibly sensitive to its surrounding environment. As the first water sign of the zodiac, this season is very much about tending to our emotional security and making sure we are in touch with our inner self and its needs. Cancer is often misjudged for its sensitivities—it's one of the most protective signs. Think of the power that the tides possess as they crash against shore. Symbolized by the Crab, it also has built-in armor. In this season, we may become more aware of who and what makes us feel safe and where we should build walls and maintain boundaries in our lives.

This is also a powerful time to look to your family's ancestry and generational patterns. We know through the study of epigenetics that trauma can be passed down through generations. Cancer season offers us the compassion to hold space for what our ancestors have gone through. If there are patterns within your family—chosen or biological—that you wish to release, now is the time to break free. All families carry some sort of baggage, and you don't need to define yourself by the past. You can choose to be better and do better. This process alone can stir up quite the emotional wave within. In turn, we may feel more emotional, nostalgic, or private. That's why it's important to slow down and prioritize solitude during this season. Being alone and rested gives us a better opportunity to connect with our intuition and inner voice as we navigate a new way forward.

During Cancer season, we likely find ourselves resisting fear of missing out and spending more time at home or with loved ones. This is a time of year in which we crave intimacy and depth in our connections. We want to bare our souls with another and invest in relationships that can stand the test of time. It's time to create the family we always desired—whether that's with our partners, best friends, community, or colleagues at work. At this time of year more than any other, the ebbs and flows of our emotional wavelength mimic the way the moon changes phases and signs multiple times throughout the week, and we feel no need to resist this. In the season of the Crab, we welcome our emotions with a judgment-free embrace. Cancer season's magick resides in our ability to tend to and validate the needs of our inner self.

SELF-CARE TIPS FOR CANCER SEASON

Feeling is Healing: Everyone is guilty of rushing through the world. There is so much pressure to be productive, when you've got deadlines to meet and engagements to attend, making the time to fully feel into your emotions can seem counterproductive. But when we allow ourselves the space to fully experience our breadth of emotions, the grip they hold over us loosens. They aren't so frightening anymore. Allowing ourselves to cry, to mourn, or to acknowledge any anger is a productive use of our time and will ultimately free up space and clear up any baggage in our subconscious.

Reorganize Your Room: Your room is your sanctuary. It's a physical expression of your sense of self. What symbols of your identity adorn your walls? What color are your sheets? By tending to your personal space, you're watering your Cancer season emotional needs for safety and security. It's a wonderful way to release stagnant energy and create a renewed sense of flow. Move your furniture around and reconsider what you surround yourself with. Is there art you could hang that is more inspiring? Could your closet benefit from some purging? Release items that resonate with an outdated version of you.

Go Down Memory Lane: Open up your yearbook or charge up one of your old iPhones and go through the photos. Flip through your old Facebook albums. Open that box with old, sentimental letters from loved ones. When we sit with past versions of ourselves, we're better able to witness our expansion and growth. Send love and gratitude for who you used to be and everything that it took to arrive at your current destination. Visiting the past can lend us perspective, because the issues we were consumed with then may seem trivial now. Nostalgia can also remind us to reestablish some lost or neglected personal connections.

YOUR LOVE LIFE + CANCER SEASON

There is no shortage of love in the world during Cancer season. Ruled by the moon, the planet that holds and expresses our emotions, we're definitely in our feels during Cancer season. Whether single or coupled, we can find ourselves reminiscing on times shared with partners present and past. We want to nurture our connection and, in return, receive the same care that we generously give. If you've been dating and are looking to take things to the next level, this is a great time to do so—whether that be by introducing your partner to your family or even moving in together.

Singles may use the waves of nostalgia that crop up during Cancer season as an opportunity to reflect on past relationship dynamics. If you still hold onto any relationships, patterns, or memories and use them as points of comparison against new potential partners, now is an aligned time to make amends and release the past once and for all. This is also a powerful time to focus on your own sense of security, safety, and stability. How can you tend to your own needs and fill your own cup? Being honest with yourself about how you appreciate being nurtured and how you define security in your relationships can lead to more confidence and a stronger foundation with your next partner(s).

Couples may crave more one-on-one time during Cancer season, when we yearn for deeper emotional connection and share pieces of our soul. Intimacy is a turn-on and so are lazy days spent at home cuddling or connecting between the sheets.

But don't be surprised if a little passive aggression also seeps into your unions. Cancer is conflict-avoidant. It sidesteps being direct like a crab and instead opts for passive jabs and comments. If you notice this pattern, it's probably time for an honest chat with your partner. Expressing yourself vulnerably, especially if it feels scary, can strengthen your bond and build a stronger sense of trust.

TRY THIS!

Plan a date night in with yourself or a partner. Order your favorite takeout and queue up your favorite flick. You can build a cozy fort in the living room, try role-playing some of your fantasies during sex or, hell, even eat your date-night dinner in bed. As you spend time focusing on your energy, take the time to be grateful for the life you've built—or are building.

HOW TO MANIFEST DURING CANCER SEASON:
RELEASE THE PAST

If you want to call in a new reality, first you must make space for it. During Cancer season, we can feel more nostalgic than normal, revisiting the past and tracing over memories or events. Because of its connection to the moon, Cancer is the zodiac sign tied to our memory. While this can be lighthearted and fun—who doesn't love reliving their highlight reel?—it's also easy to get caught up in a spiral of regret ("If I had only done or said X, things would be different"). The farther we go down this line of thinking, the further we drift from the present. As a result, we lose sight of how far we've come and what we're grateful for.

In Cancer season, we find the seeds of manifestation in the release of that which no longer serves us. It's the perfect time to use our memories as a springboard for letting go of the past so that we can manifest a more positive reality. Whether it's grief, shame, guilt, or fears, it's time to clear out emotional baggage so we can create space to birth something new. The old stories we tell ourselves are often skewed or not grounded in reality, and they tie us to a past version of ourselves that elicits shame, regret, or guilt. It's through this process of deep reflection and making the conscious decision to forgive and extend compassion to ourselves that we are able to move forward.

TRY THIS!

Grab a piece of paper and write down some of your most painful memories. The more detail the better. At the end of your petition, write, "I choose to release this story now. And so it is." Place the petition under a glass of water and charge the water by leaving it outside under the moonlight. (Bonus points if you do this after a full moon; when the moon loses light, it's an aligned time to focus on energies we want to remove from our life.) The next day, burn your piece of paper and place the ashes in the toilet. Pour the water from your glass in the toilet and flush it all together. As you flush it, repeat, "I choose to release this story now. And so it is."

CANCER SEASON **MOON MAGICK**

)) ◗ ◔ ● ● ◐ (((

Each Cancer season includes a new moon in Cancer and a full moon in Capricorn. The Cancer-Capricorn axis is all about security on both ends of the spectrum—emotional security (Cancer) and the security we build for ourselves through our ambitions, goals, and the legacy we want to leave behind (Capricorn). The days these lunations take place shift from year to year. The following ideas can help you make the most of these moonbeams.

New Moon in Cancer

It's time to get emotional! The new moon in Cancer brings in a tidal wave of emotions—and a fresh start to our private lives and foundation. Topics such as how we relate to our chosen family, our sense of security, our emotional landscape, or our living situation come into focus under this moon. New moons are portals for manifestation. As a cardinal sign, Cancer emphasizes our will and ability to act, but first we must feel. This is a great opportunity for a gratitude meditation. Find a quiet place to sit, clear your mind, and focus on what you are grateful for now. When you think of what you're grateful for, think about where you feel it in your body. You can use this feeling to amplify your manifestations under the new moon.

The moon loves to be in Cancer—it is in its true home in this zodiac sign, which means it is better able to tap into lunar qualities. The moon is comfortable in this sign—bundled up in a familiar and cozy blanket. This lends a little extra strength and ease to our manifestations; the moon packs a magical punch. The new moon in Cancer is an aligned time to renew your sense of comfort. What makes you feel safe, secure, and seen? Who ignites those feelings within you? Be sure to tend to those connections. Being in your own energy will help you ground and center. It's also important to listen to your body; if you're craving rest, rest. With our busy schedules, it's so easy to lose appreciation for the little things. Be intentional with the time you spend at home. Feel into your gratitude for having access to warm water, the cozy blanket on your couch, and the roof over your heard. Not everyone has the privilege and access to these things we often take for granted.

Full Moon in Capricorn

Capricorn energy pulls us into the future—we're concerned with our legacy, reputation, and the memory we will leave behind. Full moons mark a culmination point and, in diligent Capricorn, this lunation can mark a critical point of accomplishment or change in career. Milestones and hard work are recognized or illuminated under these moonbeams. Our relationship with our public and private lives also takes precedence. If you find yourself caring too much about other people's expectations of you, this full moon can be a reality check and invitation to call back some of your power. You deserve recognition for your hard work, yes, but at what expense? If you're reaching great achievements but working toward someone else's priorities or society's expectations of you, you may feel more inauthentic on the inside as time passes.

The full moon in Capricorn can arrive as a wakeup call and course correction. If you're not currently aligned with a meaningful path that will help you create the legacy that you truly want, it might be time to switch directions.

The balance between our personal and private lives also come into focus. Has your productivity or achievement-oriented mindset harmed some of your close relationships? If so, it's time to rebalance the scales. This full moon could also mark a period of time where you're achieving a lot, but privately sorting through some intense family matters or working on releasing the past. From the outside, your life looks great, but others are only seeing the highlight reel. We're confronted with our ideals of our future and past and must reconcile them. Where are we now and can it be enough?

Capricorn is ruled by Saturn, a hardworking and relentless planet. Lend yourself extra compassion under the full moon. It's also a powerful time to release self-criticism and pieces of your past that will hold you back from who you want to be in the future.

TRY THIS!

Use this full moon as a cosmic check-in on where you're headed. If you were on your death bed tomorrow, would you be proud of all you've accomplished? Or would you feel like you lived out someone else's dream? Don't be afraid to make dramatic changes to your life trajectory, as long as it feels authentic and aligned.

Submerge into Your Subconscious

Tapping into the water element, Cancer season's ritual involves drawing yourself a cleansing bath. In *curanderismo*, a spiritual practice that stems from various Indigenous people from Mesoamerica, *baños espirituales* are a practice you can use to cleanse yourself from unwanted energies. You may consider looking to your personal ancestry to make the most of this ritual and think about how your ancestors used the element of water to cleanse themselves spiritually. Here's a simple ritual for preparing your own cleansing bath that includes herbs that will ground, protect, and tend to our soul and to your body's emotional and physical needs.

- *Bath*
- *Prayer/intention*
- *Rosemary (3 clippings)*
- *Basil (3 leaves)*
- *Bay leaf (1)*

1. Steep the herbs in a pot of water on your stove for 30 minutes. Then strain and let cool.

2. Before hopping in the bath, write a prayer to your wise and well Spirits and ancestors—or even to the Universe if that's more comfortable. It doesn't have to be long—just a few sentences. What do you wish to ask their assistance with?

3. Draw a bath and set an intention of what you're eager to release. When you're ready, cleanse yourself with the mix of steeped herbs and pour it over your head. Then read your prayer out loud. Submerge your head three times in the bath water to fully take in the energy of your cleansing herbs.

4. Follow up with a cold shower cleanse. Rinse yourself in cold water to wash all those unwanted energies away.

5. When you step out of the shower, imagine you're entering a new reality or timeline, free of whatever you decided to release.

CANCER
AFFIRMATIONS

Empathy is my love language.

I trust my instincts and intuition.

I deserve to be nurtured the way I nurture others.

My memories are precious gifts.

I feel deeply. My love is limitless.

I listen to my body when it asks for me to rest.

My loyalty is rare.

My ancestors are protecting and watching over me.

I am compassionate.

My home is my sanctuary.

I deserve to feel safe in my environment.

There is magick in my roots.

Every time I choose to feel, I heal.

My sensitivity is one of my greatest strengths.

I release myself from the past.

Dare to take up space.

Follow your childlike joy.

Treat love as your guiding light.

CHAPTER 5

LEO SEASON

July 23–August 22

Leo season jolts us out of Cancer season's introverted mood and projects us into an entirely new stratosphere. In this season, we're feeling confident and eager to soak up the Sun. We've replenished our energetic reserves, spent enough time in our feels, and are ready to be seen! The Sun travels through Leo from approximately July 23 until August 22 and marks the height of the summer season.

Ruled by the Sun, the center of our solar system, it's no surprise that this zodiac sign adores a little attention and has a reputation for being self-centered. Leo season's magick summons us to reconnect with our inner confidence. As our confidence increases, we naturally feel more extroverted. Did someone say life of the party? Leo season coincides with the climax of summer and we're ready to be seen (in our chicest outfits) and spend time with our friends. Life becomes about play again, and we're more likely to stay out dancing past midnight or say yes to happy hours after work. It's also time to release the need for outside validation and validate ourselves. When you dare to take up space and be visible, more blessings become available! This is a good time to consider: In what ways you have been dimming your shine? Have you been playing small or acting more relatable to make others feel comfortable? It's time to let your mane out and accept praise and recognition for your own unique magick. After all, there is no one else in the Universe exactly like you!

Contrary to popular belief, a lot of Leos struggle with compliments. There's the desire for attention, sure, but once you've captivated your audience, the pressure to perform reaches new heights. This time of year can bring up reflections about your relationship with recognition. Do you accept it when it arrives? Or do you tense up and feel a tinge of panic? Recognition arrives for one simple reason: You deserve it. Leo season brings pleasure and joy back into our way of life and all that we're working toward. It makes us feel that it's safe to be seen and feel grateful for what makes us unique. It reminds us that we can be silly and childlike. Joy and pleasure are a practice and ritual. They're something to be nurtured and tended to. When we neglect pleasure for too long, it can feel foreign or like that connection is lost forever. Reconnect with whatever helps you call more joy back into your life.

Loving and generous, Leo reminds us that we are all made of love. Love is our guiding force and, when we give it freely and nurture it proactively, we can accomplish our wildest dreams. The heart is associated with Leo in astrology, and this season asks us to take inspired action from this part of ourselves. Think back to your childhood—what did you truly desire? What dreams evoked a bright, burning, exciting sensation within your heart space? It's time to release imposter syndrome or any doubts or fears and lean into the Lion's courageous spirit. It's time to release your fears around living authentically. Your quirks define your brand of magick; lean into them and meet the wisdom of Leo season.

SELF-CARE TIPS FOR LEO SEASON

Spend Time with Your Inner Child:

Close your eyes and bring up an image of your inner child to your mind's eye. What were you wearing? What toys surround you? What did your room look like? Tune into your senses and what it feels like to be in that space. Now ask your inner child, what was your biggest dream? Clear your thoughts and tune into the stream of consciousness that comes to your mind. If it's something you've experienced or accomplished, let your inner child know: "We did that."

Now, ask your inner child about something they needed but didn't receive. Attention? Recognition? More love or hugs? Visualize a beam of light emanating from your heart space and send it to their heart space. Feel into this energy until it surrounds you both. Send what they needed to them and remind them they are safe, protected, and loved. Ask them what their advice is to bring more joy into your life right now. Listen to them and do it!

Get Glammed Up:

The quickest way to tap into your unlimited source of radiance is by stepping up your glam! Playing dress-up can spur a new level of confidence from within and help you to feel into a future reality or version of yourself in the present. Is this how your future self would dress? Pretend you're about to be a guest on a talk show for something you hope to accomplish. How would you dress? Switch up your hair, outfit, and makeup to activate this new reality. The more you can physically feel into that state, the quicker it will manifest in reality.

Go Out:

Leo loves to be the center of attention, and getting ready to go out with friends can reawaken some of your inner confidence. Lions live in prides, and Leo is a social sign. Spending time with friends and loved ones—while embodying the most glamourous version of yourself—will recharge your batteries during this season.

YOUR LOVE LIFE + LEO SEASON

Bring on the public displays of affection! We're going big during Leo season and ready to accept every compliment and more. Leo has over-the-top energy and doesn't shy away from the spotlight. This is the time for grand displays of affection, especially if you want everyone to know how much you adore your partner or partners. We also want our partners to recognize our inner light and what makes us uniquely special.

Singles, meanwhile, can find themselves entering a sexy selfie era. This is a great use of Leo energy: Don't be afraid to strike a pose and show all your exes what they're missing. This is the best time to let your confidence shine brightly and boldly.

Leo season is all about aligning with your heart's authentic desires. Are you in a relationship that meets other people's expectations, or are you actually fulfilled? When the Lion takes over the skies, we are more courageous; we move and act boldly with our heart's interests in mind. Ruled by the heart, at its core Leo craves the carefree joy and fun from childhood at every twist and turn. We want to feel energized and inspired by our connections. What is the point of love if we can't have fun together? We're reminded to lead with the heart and take life less seriously. Leo season is a great time to combine activities from your childhood with date nights—go mini golfing, go-kart racing, or try out a paint night.

Leo loves a dose of drama, which can also enter our romantic sphere during Leo season. We crave excitement and can sometimes get carried away, overdramatizing situations and making mountains out of molehills. If we have creative outlets and new experiences to share with the people we love, this tendency for theatrics can be more easily tempered and managed.

TRY THIS!

Put on something reflective or shiny. Leo season is notorious for drawing in all types of attention—especially unwanted and jealous admirers. Wearing a reflective object is a glamour magick tip that will help you reflect anyone else's uninvited energy and return them to the sender.

HOW TO MANIFEST DURING LEO SEASON: MIRROR MAGICK

Leo may have an over-the-top (and pretty valid) reputation for being self-obsessed, but a little self-love never hurt anyone! Plus there is something empowering about holding eye contact with yourself in a mirror. And, believe it or not, you can use that to access a realm of unlimited potential and magick.

Mirror magick is one of the quickest ways to improve your self-talk and bring your desires Earth-side. You can use your reflection as a portal to speak about your future reality in detail and pretend that your reflection is that version of yourself. We're also going to pair this with emotional freedom technique (EFT) tapping, or psychological acupressure, to root into our physical body and experience our future while we speak it. In a 2019 study in the *National Library of Medicine Journal,* EFT tapping was shown to improve multiple physiological markers of health, including stress reduction. It helps create new neural pathways and associations within the mind.

In this manifestation practice, look into a mirror and stare deeply into your eyes, connecting with your energy on the other side of the mirror. Bring to mind a desire that you hope to manifest. Use both hands to tap on the following points: the top of your head, above your eyebrows, the sides of your eyes, under your eyes, under your nose, on your chin, on your collarbones, under your armpit (one hand), and then tap the inside of your wrists together. At each tapping point, describe a different aspect of your future reality in the present tense, as if it's already transpired.

To make the most of this experience, use affirmations that evoke your physical senses. What do you look like in this timeline? How do you feel? What tastes, smells, and textures bring you joy? Then move into the specific goals—what do you want to accomplish and why? If you can't name a reason why, it's almost like the goal doesn't have any footing. Really feel into what this means to you and how it impacts your existence, as well as others. This process will leave you feeling closer to your desires and charge you with an energized spark to take action with unshakable confidence.

LEO SEASON **MOON MAGICK**

)) ◗ ● ● ● ◖ ((

Each Leo season includes a new moon in Leo and a full moon in Aquarius. The individual and the individual's place within groups or society are topics highlighted under the Leo-Aquarius axis. The days these lunations take place shift from year to year. The following ideas can help you make the most of these cosmic shifts.

New Moon in Leo

This is your cosmic check-in—are you living authentically? The new moon in Leo asks you to tend to your joy, passion, and leisure. What pursuits does your heart crave? Leo's confidence dares us to be different; we're not afraid to self-express and take up space. The new moon in Leo delivers a new beginning regarding our identity and sense of self. How can you lean deeper into appreciation for your own eccentricities? It's only when we embrace every part of ourselves that we can truly embody a new level of confidence.

This is also a profound time to check in with your heart. What does it want to achieve, and who does it want? Are you living in alignment with your internal compass and desires? This is the time to set intentions around your relationship with your confidence and need for recognition. Choose to validate yourself. Let your own opinion and feelings about who you are outweigh the chattering opinions of others. When we break free from the limiting shackles of adulthood and the expectations of others, we are free to follow our heart's desires.

The new moon in Leo is perfect for setting a creative goal. Think back to your inner artist or creative as a child; what activities did you treasure? Don't be afraid to take up space and enjoy your time centerstage. Give yourself the room for failure, because it means you were courageous enough to try! Wherever you have abandoned your needs and desires, the new moon in Leo reminds you that they matter. Take time for yourself and prioritize your wishes so you can leave your mark on this world.

Full Moon in Aquarius

The full moon in Aquarius reminds us of the relationship between pursuing our needs as opposed to working together as a collective. You might ask yourself, where do I need to find more balance between pursuing my goals and ambitions on my own, and where do I need to suck it up and ask for help? Collaborations of all kinds can lead to breakthroughs.

A team effort may come to fruition under this lunation. Aquarius is a social sign that encourages us to reflect on the groups we are part of. Who do we invest our time with? Where do we feel a sense of community and feel like we belong? This lunation can have us feeling gratitude for those spaces and communities or bring important realizations about how we need to alter our social sphere accordingly.

Ruled by serious Saturn, the full moon in Aquarius brings up boundaries. This moon may illuminate situations where you need to set clear expectations. A Saturn-ruled moon reminds us that our time is limited and worth protecting. A Saturn-ruled moon can also bring our attention to the collective. Aquarius cares about society and the future. It's an innovative and progressive sign that is concerned with how we treat one another. Its connection with limits and boundaries makes it well-aware of what lies beyond the boundaries of society. How do the rules and structures we put in place affect those on the fringes of society? It's always important to reflect on outdated and harmful societal structures, but under this moon you may hear the need for change loud and clear. Rebellion is in the air under these moonbeams, and you may also feel called to move in a different way or release an outdated way of being.

TRY THIS!

If you're able, find an organization that means something to you and apply to volunteer. Donating your time and energy to help others is usually a positive experience.

Soak Up the Sun

The Sun, the center of our solar system and Leo's ruling planet, represents our vitality. It's a major part of sustaining our life, which is why many cultures worship the Sun and respect it as a deity. The best way to make the most of Leo season is to take the time to be grateful for the Lion's ruling planet with a daily Sun-worshipping practice.

This ritual is inspired by ancient Mesoamerica practices, where the Mexica and Maya maintained daily Sun-worshipping rituals. They interacted with the Sun multiple times a day and believed that the Sun was our main source of lifeforce energy, also known as *tonalli*. Interacting with the Sun's rays at various times of the day had assorted symbolic meanings—dawn was for rebirth, sunrise was for manifestation, morning for cleansing, and so on. Curandera Erika Buenaflor, M.A., J.D., details the history and significance of these various Sun-worshipping rituals in her book *Sacred Energies of the Sun & Moon: Shamanic Rites of Curanderismo*.

1. Step outside, squat, and place your palms on the ground. Close your eyes, and raise your head toward the sky. Feel the Sun's rays beating on your forehead and infusing your body with warmth.

2. As you do this, send a beam of gratitude up through your crown chakra back to the Sun. Name the ways in which the Sun enhances your life and cares for you. Ask for its assistance in bringing some of your desires Earth-side. What do you need to get to where you want to be: More confidence? More discipline? As you feel the Sun's heat warming your body, imagine it is infusing you with those qualities.

3. When you feel ready, sit comfortably on the ground for five minutes absorbing the sun's rays. Repeat this three times a day: in the morning, at noon, and before sunset.

LEO
AFFIRMATIONS

It is safe for me to take up space.

I shine so bright.

My authenticity is my superpower.

My inner child knows best.

I radiate confidence.

Having fun is my job.

There is no one else in the world like me.

I love every part of me—the good, the bad, and the ugly.

I choose to validate myself.

I am a conduit for creativity.

I lead with my heart.

My generosity is contagious.

I am a ray of light.

My generosity always comes back to me.

Making time for play and pleasure is a radical and restorative act.

I always choose love.

My generosity brings me blessings.

Perfectionism is a myth; embrace the mess and the process.

Declutter your space and your mind.

Find magick in the mundane.

CHAPTER 6

VIRGO SEASON

August 23–September 20

We let loose during Leo season, but Virgo season is here to help us get grounded. Everyone knows Virgos are meticulous and detail-oriented and have a keen eye for organization. If there's a system, there's a way! Running from approximately August 23 through September 20, Virgo season is the perfect time to get our ducks in a row. Think of back-to-school season—sharpening pencils and labeling binders and notebooks. You want all the tools you'll need ready to go.

Virgo is represented by the Maiden and is often depicted holding a blade of wheat. As an earth sign, Virgo and the Maiden are connected to the harvest. Once we reach Virgo, we are halfway through the zodiac; the seeds we planted at the beginning of the year are ready to harvest. Virgo is also associated with purity—the Maiden is true to herself and has a strong moral compass.

Similar to Gemini, Virgo is ruled by Mercury, the planet of the mind. If Gemini is about gathering the facts, Virgo is all about the assessment of information. As the editor in the zodiac, this sign is about refining what needs to stay and what can go. A physical purge of our living spaces, driving spaces, and work spaces can help to clear mental clutter. We're thinking back to goals we set at the beginning of spring as we almost meet our halfway mark around the zodiac wheel. It's time to refine our plans and examine our next steps.

All the same, we must be careful to not overthink. Mercury's influence on the season can usher in a wave of self-criticism. If you've been finding yourself wandering down a wormhole of negative beliefs or self-talk, it's time to hit mute on your inner voice. While Virgo has a reputation for being a perfectionist, this season calls us to move away from that standard. Perfectionism is an unattainable standard. Rather than obsess over where we "fall short," we can use these feelings of inadequacy that are bound to come up during Virgo season as a reminder to be gentler with ourselves. Zoom in on areas of your life where you're putting too much pressure on yourself and use these smoke signals as a call to be a little kinder to yourself as you move throughout the season. No one has all the answers or the perfect solution; we're all just doing our best.

Virgo feels most useful and validated when being in service to others. During Leo season, we recognize our unique gifts and talents. Virgo season asks us to go a step further and think about how we can use our strengths to make an impact and help others. It's not enough to be recognized for something—the real meaning comes from sharing our individual abilities with others. Virgo is also no stranger to self-improvement, and through the process of self-exploration and healing, it's picked up some life-changing tools along the way. What wisdom do you have that could benefit others? Virgo yearns to be of service and to leave the world better than we found it. Virgo season is concerned with giving back and knows that we feel the most whole and connected when we're at our most selfless.

**Purge +
Donate:**	Make a list of all the rooms in your house. Start with one room each weekend. Go through the room—every drawer, nook, and cranny. Create a pile of items that you can recycle, donate, or throw away. (Obviously we'd love to reduce trash and our carbon imprint for the environment's sake, so lean toward recycling and donating when possible.) The purpose is twofold: First, to witness how much abundance you do have—you'll probably come across a few items you forgot you had, and second, to clear out clutter and free up space. This physical opening of your space will open space in your mind, making more room for what is useful and removing what isn't.
Volunteer:	Virgo is one of the most selfless zodiac signs—they live to serve. Think about a cause or organization that is meaningful to you. Not all of us are privileged with the time or resources to volunteer, but if it is possible for you, volunteer at an organization that aligns with your values. Giving back and contributing to the community in a way that feels fulfilling will deepen your sense of purpose. When we pay it forward, we gain new perspective through selfness acts and, as an added bonus, the Universe also sends some blessings our way.
**Change One
Habit:**	Pick one habit that you've been talking about changing for months or years—morning meditation, working out, integrating more greens into your diet, a daily walk, a skincare routine, reading before bed—it truly doesn't matter what the habit is just that you have a desire to approach it in a new way. Start small and temper your expectations. When we make a list of all the habits we want to change, it's so easy to get overwhelmed. But if we start with one and set aside a 10-minute window to engage consistently, it's not difficult to build endurance as we slowly shift our behaviors. When we feel into the success of shifting this habit, it will become easier to make other changes in our lives moving forward, too.

YOUR LOVE LIFE + VIRGO SEASON

Keep it simple! Virgo season's expression of love is a drastic departure from Leo season's fireworks. We're going back to the basics and interested in honoring and cherishing the little moments with one another. There is a big emphasis on listening during Virgo season. We appreciate when someone remembers the little things about ourselves that we've dropped into casual conversation—like bringing home our favorite chocolate bar from the grocery store unprompted. Our heart skips a beat over all of the little things and small acts of service. We crave affection in our everyday life, and sometimes the best way to do that is by showing up and supporting the natural ebbs and flow of daily life. It doesn't sound super sexy at first, but if you think about it, what's sexier than coming home to an unloaded dishwasher and freshly folded laundry after a long day of work? After all, by the time you do find yourself in bed with your lover, you'll have nothing running through your mind to distract you.

Virgo season's passion exists in the little moments—passing each other in the kitchen and grabbing one another's butts. Holding hands while you Netflix and chill. A nice back scratch after a long and tiring day. Small acts of service and affection keep the spark alive. We're also interested in blending our routines together—do you share similar interests or a compatible lifestyle? When we feel in flow with our partner, it's one less thing we need to worry about. There's harmony in the household and it can once again be a safe space. We know what to expect.

During Virgo season, we've also got planning on our minds. What do we want for our shared future? How will we get there? Communication becomes key, thanks to Mercury as Virgo's ruling planet. Whether single or coupled, you might find it easier during Virgo season to express what you truly want from a loving relationship. Don't be afraid to speak your mind; it can lead to a healthier union! We're also a little more critical and discerning in matters of the heart during this season. Virgo energy is very giving, so be sure to ask yourself, *Is this person worth the investment?*

Virgo is the sign of self-improvement. Singles can use this season's energy to focus on streamlining their own personal routines and habits. While this doesn't sound particularly romantic or sexy, when we feel in flow and are actively engaging in activities that support our mental, physical, spiritual, and psychic wellbeing, we project ourselves differently into the world, our aura radiates with a new light, and we are better able to attract others who are in alignment with the lifestyle we wish to lead. Singles may also find that they meet potential partners checking off chores on our to do list like while at the grocery store, picking up a prescription, or attending a workout class at the gym.

TRY THIS!

As unsexy as this conversation sounds, couples who divvy up the chores tend to be more content. Discussing your expectations around housework, cooking, yardwork and so on will lead to less built-up resentment in the long run.

Virgo knows it best—there is magick to be found in every area of our lives. Believe it or not, you don't need crystals, a cauldron, candles, oils, and more to tap into some serious life-altering magick. Our personal grooming habits, and daily routine offer us plenty of opportunities to shift our reality. The root of most magical practices is discipline and consistency. Virgo season reminds us that when we integrate a new habit into our routine, the little ripples we experience right away eventually grow into powerful waves.

Here are some everyday actions that you can pair with a magical intention to kickstart your dream life:

- **Grooming:** If you're struggling to let go of a desire you're trying to manifest repeat "I release my desire" as you cut your nails. You can also use this to shake a limiting belief; just focus on what you want to cut out of your life. The same can be said if you are someone who shaves any part of your body. As you shave, repeat what you are releasing out loud and watch the hair drift down the drain.
- **Eliminating Waste:** When you go to the bathroom, associate what you're doing with energetic release. What limiting belief or anxiety are you ready to remove? Visualize the words in your head, and as the waste exits your body and you flush the toilet, imagine those thoughts or feelings as good as gone.
- **Bathing:** Whether you're washing your hair or lathering your skin with soap, visualize scrubbing off unwanted energies. As you rinse, watch the soap leave your body and swirl down the drain. Visualize any lingering energetic attachments leaving your energy field.
- **Cooking:** Try shifting your thinking and bringing in more abundance or positivity in your life while cooking. As you add ingredients to your meal, associate them with specific traits like confidence, courage, or consistency. When you eat your meal, imagine you are ingesting those qualities and move forward as such.
- **Cleaning:** Our living space is often reflective of our mental state. As you clean and organize, pair those activities with an intention for more clarity and spaciousness. This can reduce anxiety and release clutter in the mind. With a smaller to-do list, it's easier activate a state of flow.
- **Getting Dressed:** As you get dressed, associate each piece of clothing with something you're trying to call in. As you layer the pieces on your body, imagine yourself putting on a physical representation of your desires or characteristics you want to embody more effortlessly.

VIRGO SEASON **MOON MAGICK**

Each Virgo season includes a new moon in Virgo and a full moon in Pisces. The Virgo-Pisces axis asks us to reflect on our relationships with both the magical and the mundane. The days these lunations take place shift from year to year. The following ideas can help you make the most of these lunations.

New Moon in Virgo

The new moon in Virgo is an opportunity to get our shit together! Though we may be preparing for fall, this lunation is like a mini New Year. As we set intentions, we are called to focus on our daily routine, habits, and health. Where do you seek to improve your life? It's the tiniest adjustments that often create the biggest ripple effects of change. When you commit to change on a small scale, you show the Universe that not only can you handle change you are ready to embrace it.

This is also a period of time to feel into the gratitude of how far we've come. We're almost halfway around the zodiac wheel, and the seeds we planted during Aries season are nearly ready for harvesting. Now, it's time to focus on strategies and structures that support the final leg of our manifestation journey. Virgo's magick is precise and no-nonsense. What are the practical steps you need to take to further your visions and goals? Virgos are the planners of the zodiac, so don't be afraid to get detailed and granular. Your specificity will speed up your desires.

TRY THIS!

Make a list of actions that will help bring your desire Earth-side. Ruled by communication planet Mercury, the new moon in Virgo favors the written word. Using checklists as an organization tool during Virgo season or the new moon in Virgo can also help you stay organized and on task.

Full Moon in Pisces

Compassion is in the air! Coming through in the emphatic water sign of Pisces, this full moon offers a portal for healing. What pieces of your past are you ready to release? Extend the compassion, grace, and care to yourself that you so willingly give to others. This lunation will bring you closer to your emotions—especially avoided emotions—but in the process, you may experience transcendence and healing. You may feel more connected to other realms and feel like you're witnessing the mysteries of the Universe in real time. Intuition is on high alert, so tune into messages from the Universe. Your guides and spirt team are communicating with you through symbols, songs, animals, or dreams.

All full moons signal a release or culmination point, so this can certainly manifest as an emotional milestone. Ruled by expansive Jupiter, Pisces knows no bounds; if you've been overextending yourself personally or professionally, this full moon can be wake-up call. Where have you been too lax with your boundaries? We are being asked to adjust our work-life balance. "No" is a complete sentence. Honoring your boundaries, while momentarily uncomfortable, will actually bring you closer to your dream life.

As one of the most creative signs, the Pisces full moon can also mark the accomplishment of a creative endeavor or inspire the creative process. As the last sign in the zodiac, it also asks us to reflect on our solitude, grief, and closing out a cycle. Pisces' guidance is simple: When you choose to consciously surrender and trust, you can free yourself from any fault, shame, or negative energy you've been carrying that is limiting your potential. What are you ready to leave behind so you can have more space for aligned opportunities or interactions in the future?

Wipe Away Your Fears

A little-known fact is that Virgo is one of the witchiest zodiac signs. Virgo exists in a realm of ritual and routine. Most spells or magical practices require dedication and committed rituals. In true Virgo season fashion, we're going to lean into an everyday task and make the mundane magical. During Virgo season we're getting our life back in order and giving our surrounding environment a good cleansing. When we pair our cleansing practices with an intention, we can bring that essence and energy into the physical world. Here's how to make a magically infused all-purpose cleanser that will clear out limiting beliefs, fears, anxiety, and what no longer serves us. In the process, we're able to freshen our environment and call in more abundance.

- *Multi-surface, eco-friendly cleaning spray*
- *Clear, glass spray bottle*
- *Rosemary (4 clippings)*
- *Cinnamon sticks (4)*
- *Water*

1. Grab a bottle of eco-friendly all-purpose cleanser and pour some of the contents into a clear, glass spray bottle until it's about three-quarters of the way full (we're going for potion jar vibes here!).

2. Steep the rosemary clippings along with the cinnamon sticks in a bowl or jar of hot water for 30 minutes. Let the mixture cool, then pour it in with the cleaning spray.

3. As you use your cleansing spray to clean your floor and the surfaces in your home, visualize the spray evaporating your limiting beliefs. Imagine you are clearing out any belief, habit, or pattern that no longer serves you. As a result, you're creating fresh space for more aligned opportunities, routines, and abundance.

VIRGO
AFFIRMATIONS

I choose to release perfectionism.

My daily habits make the most significant changes in my life.

I honor my boundaries.

I am compassionate.

Slow and steady wins the race.

My hard work will be rewarded.

"No" is a complete sentence.

I am grateful to be of service and share my gifts with others.

I am always improving and upgrading my life.

The more organized I am, the more flow there is in my life.

My imperfections make me unique and beautiful.

My self-criticism doesn't define me.

My ingenuity always leads me to solutions.

Accepting help from others is not a weakness.

My attention to detail takes me far in life.

Embrace your inner social butterfly.

Experiment with your art and style.

Walk down Lovers Lane.

CHAPTER 7

LIBRA SEASON

September 21–October 22

The leaves begin to change colors and the air is crisp. Libra season takes over the skies roughly from September 21 through October 22 and makes its entrance with an attention-grabbing spectacle: the Fall Equinox. Virgo season prepared us for change, and now it's time to embrace it. The Fall Equinox is similar to the Vernal Equinox in that, on this date, day and night are of equal length. After this, in the Northern Hemisphere, the Sun will begin to lose its dominance as the days shorten and the nights grow longer. Winter is coming. The equinox marks a point of self-reflection— to look back at our harvest and how far we've come since spring. Symbolized by the Scales, Libra's desire for balance and harmony is something we tangibly experience on this date as the Sun and shadow share equal parts of our lives.

The Fall Equinox reminds us that the shadow is equally as important as the light. That message ties into Libra's quest for equity and justice—this zodiac sign wants to even the Scales for everyone. Libra has a reputation for being superficial, but this is a misunderstanding. There is much wisdom in this sign. Libra can recognize the beauty in the multi-colored fall leaves and also acknowledge the decay that's to come. There is great depth that comes with Libra. With a massive amount of effort spent weighing pros and cons, Libra lands on the right decision.

During Libra season, it's an important time to check in with what you stand for and your privilege and position in the world. It's a good time to think about how you can leverage who you are and what you can access to make the world a better place. Though not exclusive to Libra season, we should prioritize these reflections this time of year.

With Venus—the planet of values, beauty, harmony, and justice—as their guiding planet, Libra's interests are varied. Libra is an artist, creative, intellectual, radical, and a style icon all wrapped up into one sign. This means there's much to celebrate and enjoy during Libra season. It's also important to remember that, with Libra, we've made it to the halfway mark of the zodiac wheel. Now is the time to pause and reflect back on the first six months of the year—look how far you've come! Don't neglect to celebrate your growth.

With Venus guiding us, we're ready to lighten the mood from always-five-steps-ahead-of-you Virgo season and engage in some more socializing and fun. Libra season highlights our connections and ability to collaborate. Our dynamics and interactions with others create a mirror effect—reflecting pieces of ourselves back to us that we may normally overlook or underestimate. This can be one of our greatest sources for understanding, self-compassion, and transformation.

Love and relationships are always on Libra's mind (let's not forget Libra's planet Venus also represents love!), and during this season we may find ourselves contemplating our various partnerships—whether that's familial, romantic, platonic, or work-oriented. Collaboration and tactful self-expression are keys to making this season successful. As an air sign, Libra season's qualities lean toward the intellectual. We're contemplating our relationships with the world around us and the people with whom we choose to spend our time and energy. With six seasons down, and six to go, it's time to reflect, refine, and integrate that wisdom moving forward.

SELF-CARE TIPS FOR LIBRA SEASON

Pros + Cons Lists:	Libra energy thrives on an old-fashioned pros and cons list. Select an area of your life where you're struggling to make a decision. Distill the issue to a concise sentence, then make two columns and create a pros and cons list. Then go through your con list and highlight any that feel like they come from a sense of fear or insecurity. See if you can rewrite that con and add it to your pro list. If not, take stock of which column is longer. Feel into your gut as you do this. What comes up? Where do you notice a physical sensation in your body next? Pair your rational takeaways from the pros and cons list with the gut feeling in your body and make a decision.
Take Yourself on a Date:	You don't have to wait for someone to come and sweep you off your feet—get up and take action now! Sure, love is in the air during Libra season, but falling deeper in love with yourself and your interests is just as important as finding a romantic relationship. Tend to your intellectual amusements—through art, culture, dance, and social interaction. Spoil yourself with new experiences.
Be Careful of People-Pleasing:	Libra is a sign that loves to placate and avoid confrontation. It's really easy to get caught up in people-pleasing tendencies. Confrontation is necessary for growth, and you deserve to advocate for your needs. Embrace the temporary discomfort of advocating for yourself; it will open more doors for you in the long run.

YOUR LOVE LIFE + LIBRA SEASON

Love and romance are often overhyped during Libra season. True, this season is very focused on relationships, but no relationship is perfect. It can't be all rainbows and butterflies. Libra reminds us that there is a shadow side in every relationship and invites us to consider how this might be playing out in our own connections. Some things that may come up during this time include self-sabotaging behaviors, residual pain, hurt, or frustration from past attachments, or the fear that comes from loving someone. Libra season offers us the space and opportunity to reflect on both the light and dark side of love. When we are honest about our fears and relationship patterns that don't serve us or no longer serve us, we can move forward with healthier dynamics.

Considering Libra's status as an initiating cardinal sign—as well as the increased desire for connection that can manifest at this time—Libra season can be a great time to update your dating profile and get back into the dating pool. Represented by the element of air, Libra has the ability to detach from situations and take on a lighthearted, breezy attitude when it comes to matters of the heart. Couples may enjoy group dates and socializing with friends or participating in activities like visiting an archery range or hosting a game night. We all benefit from reflecting on collaborative efforts and considering how our input affects the output. How do we work with others? This season is a good time to find out!

This is the time of year to balance the scales and redefine stability in all of our associations. Do you fall into patterns of seeking outside approval and putting everyone else above your needs? In romance, do you and your partner contribute to the union in fair, meaningful, and positive ways? At home, is the responsibility of the household falling heavily on one person? This is the time to work toward equilibrium.

HOW TO MANIFEST DURING LIBRA SEASON: ABSORB ART

When left unwatered, the creative rivers and ravines running through our minds dry up. Spending time honing our imagination and creative skills—through painting, dancing, writing or whatever else moves you—helps strengthen the capacity to dream big. Libra loves to absorb art and beauty in any form. Tending to our intellect and curiosity through various mediums and social events can lead to mental expansion. Libra season asks you to sign up for a dance class you've considered or finish the novel on your nightstand. You never know who you'll meet or what quote you'll read that could inspire a wildfire within. Our ability to focus on the various ways beauty surrounds us now brings us back to the present. We're better able to adopt a carefree spirit as we move through the world. When we appreciate our blessings and those we can see, hear or read about, we live in the moment rather than chasing some version of happiness in the future.

Collaboration and working with others are also other ways to experience a speedup of your manifestations during Libra season. Asking others for their perspective and creative input can oftentimes reveal the final piece of the puzzle. It won't make your work any less yours—consider asking for a second set of eyes on what you're working toward or seeking advice from someone you trust about what next steps to take.

TRY THIS!

Socializing during Libra season is a must; get a group together and practice a manifestation exercise together. The more minds working together to envision a desire and goal, the better. Before engaging in a guided meditation and visualization practice, go around the room and tell one another what you're hoping to call in. Sharing this with others will allow everyone else to visualize and feel into your dream, charging it with more energy. Then select a guided meditation and focus on your individual intention as you sit together.

)) ◗ ● ● ● ◖ ((

Each Libra season includes a new moon in Libra and a full moon in Aries. The Aries-Libra axis encapsulates our will to move forward and desire to establish harmony and equilibrium. The days these lunations take place shift each year. The following ideas can help you make the most of these powerful cosmic events.

New Moon in Libra

It's everyone's favorite season—cuffing season! The new moon in Libra ushers in a Lovers Lane vibe. It's time to set intentions around love and partnerships. If focusing on a romantic relationship isn't a priority—that's no problem. Libra new moons focus on collaboration at their core. Who do we wish to work with and share our magick with? This is an aligned time to send pitches to businesses or people you'd like to partner or work with. Contracts signed around this time can also signal an ongoing joint relationship.

In general, we're re-evaluating our relationship with balance. Is there an area in your life that has veered too far in one direction? Now is the time to find your footing again. This yearly lunation also asks us to think about harmony within our closest ties. Think about where you're giving too much or perhaps receiving too little. Boundaries are also up for review—have you been too lax with yours? We've made it through half of the astrological year, and this is the first new moon as we move through the second half of the zodiac. What are you grateful for, and where do you go from here? This is a time of reassessment, too. How has your journey around the zodiac wheel informed how you would like to move forward? Have your priorities and desires shifted? Refine accordingly. Libra's cardinal energy gives you the momentum to take action and move forward with confidence.

Full Moon in Aries

If Libra season is all about recalibrating harmony and balance within our lives, the full moon in Aries really shakes up our foundation! This lunation is an invitation to get comfortable with your anger. You're asked to stand your ground in all of your unions. If simmering resentments and frustrations have built up, now is the time to address those. Engaging in physical activities is recommended during the full moon in Aries; it's a wonderful way to channel and express your rage in a healthy way. Let's not forget the Sun's position is still hovering in the sign of Libra, so we're asked to release any anger with tact and with the intention of finding more congruence in our associations.

This is our first full moon as we traverse the second-half of the zodiac. Remember spring when we planted seeds during the new moon in Aries? It's time to discover what has grown from those seeds! This spotlight moment brings a culmination of your manifestation and will. What were you calling in back in Aries season, and how much closer are you to it now? If the seeds you planted haven't sprouted, maybe it is time for you to release your original goal, reimagine it, and course-correct accordingly.

Self-Love Spell

Everyone is intrigued by a good love spell! The truth about manifesting love is that the most effective place to start is always with your relationship to yourself. When we focus on attracting more self-love, as a side effect we often experience a newfound wave of romance in our lives. You can also use this ritual to call in more harmony in your established union or release any discord that's been building in your partnerships.

- *Rose quartz*
- *Rose petals*
- *Tealight candle*

1. Turn your nightstand into an altar or use a special altar within your home. Adorn it with rose petals (which are associated with love and bounty) and set your intentions.

2. Lay down on your bed or near your altar, place your rose quartz on your heart, and tune in to your breath. Shift your mind into a less active state (use a guided meditation on YouTube or an app if it's helpful). Feel into the rose quartz's weight on your chest as you breathe in and out.

3. As you exhale, imagine releasing old relationship stories that tie you to the past. As you inhale, focus on a wave of love moving through your being, starting at your crown and moving down your neck, through your core, and extending beyond your feet. Once you feel this tingling sensation, repeat, "I am safe. I am loved. I am protected."

4. Repeat this ritual nightly during this season. Place your rose quartz back on its altar and light the candle. Tend to your altar like a living being; replace the flower petals as they die and switch out your candle once it burns out. Let the light from the candle remind you of the regenerative and limitless loving light within you.

LIBRA
AFFIRMATIONS

I maintain balance in all areas of my life.

I consider other's opinions.

We are all made of love.

*When I surround myself with beauty, I experience more
ease and harmony in my life.*

Collaboration inspires me in new ways.

I seek justice for all.

I choose a peaceful way of being.

I am charming and magnetic.

My internal beauty shines through.

My desires desire me.

My connections with others help me grow and evolve.

I appreciate both the light and the dark within me.

My style is sensational and iconic.

I take action for the highest good of all involved.

Plunge into the depths of your personal darkness and embrace it.

Release the need for control.

Let your sixth sense be your guide.

CHAPTER 8

SCORPIO SEASON

October 23–November 21

Grab your flashlight—it's time to venture into the dark waters of Scorpio season. During Libra season, we focused on nurturing our connections; now Scorpio season asks us to confront the unknown and our fears that bubble to the surface when we dare to be vulnerable, intimate, and entangled with another soul. Scorpio season sweeps across the sky roughly from October 23 through November 21. As a water sign, Scorpio is naturally emotional, intuitive, and sensitive.

Scorpio is represented by the Scorpion, equipped with a tough exoskeleton and quick stinger that reminds us of Scorpio's defensive and protective nature, as well as its innate power. Scorpions also live and thrive in harsh climates–reflecting Scorpio's resilience in challenging, external circumstances.

Scorpio season is the time to survey our emotional landscape and explore what we've been hiding or avoiding beneath the surface. During this time, as the Sun continues to lose light in the Northern Hemisphere, there is an understanding of what awaits: decay and darkness. This season invites us to tap into our deep well of power to sit with our emotions rather than avoid them. This is the season to face our fears and, in the process, anticipate transformation.

Scorpio season asks us to reflect on our relationship with control. Our own resistance and desire to control certain situations can be a self-fulfilling prophecy. Often, the place where we've been holding on too tightly is where we need to surrender and step away the most. Scorpio—ruled by Mars, the planet of sex, action, and war—is strategic in how it exerts its energetic reserves. There is no half-assing anything during Scorpio season; we are here for the extremes. Scorpio season reminds us to be grateful for our shadow—for light and darkness share a symbiotic bond and rely on one another. Remember, it is the light that creates our shadow. Just because Scorpio is associated with intensity and endings, doesn't mean death is around the corner. The true magick of Scorpio season lies in our ability to transmute our pain and alchemize it into gold. Scorpio season reminds us of our resilience— and that pain can be a great teacher. You're a survivor. Every part of you and your story—no matter how complicated or contradictory—matters.

As a fixed sign, Scorpio has focused precision that lends us the determination to see our dreams through, even when we experiencing a crisis. We learn the power of duality—that light cannot exist without dark and that a new beginning is around the corner of every ending. It's time to exercise your discernment and defend your time and energy. We're more ambitious during Scorpio season, which will require more forethought and more calculation before taking action. Your power, depth, and loyalty should be reserved for those who recognize and appreciate every part of you—not just the taboo-free parts. When you initiate a tough conversation and or choose to do something that scares you, Scorpio season reminds you that transformation is imminent. Your personal phoenix moment is here. With tenacious courage and a commitment to tackling your fears, you will be rewarded. At the end of the tunnel, there is light.

Spend Time with Your Shadow:	It's easy for us to acknowledge the parts of ourselves that we are proud of and that represent how we hope to be perceived by the world. But in doing so, we can remain stagnant or stuck. When we spend time with our shadow, or the parts of ourselves that we reject and shame, we experience a new level of self-love, self-compassion, and self-forgiveness. Pay attention to behaviors in others that trigger you and ask yourself, *In what ways do I reject these pieces of myself?* Make a regular practice of sending love to the parts of you that you'd rather keep hidden; they deserve to be seen.
Schedule Time to Grieve:	Grief isn't linear, and some wounds never fully heal. In a capitalistic society that places so much focus on achievement, it can be difficult to slow down and spend time with painful emotions that threaten to derail us from our productivity. Yet, our pain can be a profound teacher. Our darker feelings, shameful memories, sense of loss, and regrets all serve a purpose; they remind us that we're human and we are worthy and deserving of learning, growing, and trying again. Taking time to journal or sit with a painful piece of your past can nurture your soul, clear out what you've been carrying around in your subconscious, and release the power that painful memories have over you.
Practice Trust + Embrace Vulnerability:	Scorpio—armed with its stinger and ready to strike—is a sign associated with defensiveness. Yet vulnerability is one of our greatest strengths and assets. When we examine our relationship with control and surrender and take emotional risks, transformation becomes possible. Learning to trust can be a cathartic and heart-opening experience. While it can be difficult to let your guard down if you've been harmed in the past, Scorpio season reminds us of the power of regeneration. Trust and share openly and honestly and, from the ashes, something beautiful will rise.

YOUR LOVE LIFE + SCORPIO SEASON

It's time to make an appointment for matching tattoos—love during Scorpio season is everlasting, intense, and passionate. Ruled by lusty Mars, the planet often associated with sex, it's no wonder Scorpio's magnetism is off the charts. Scorpio asks us to bare our souls when it comes to love. Scorpio season can be steamy and may bring out your hornier side. That said, sex is much more than a physical act; it's sacred and connection is key. It's time to investigate your fears, as well as what's been holding you back in your love. Shadow qualities of Scorpio are often depicted as possessive, jealous, and paranoid; from this perspective, Scorpio season is a divine time to reflect on the power dynamics within your closest connections. You deserve to feel safe enough to be vulnerable with your loved ones—and to clear out what's been getting in the way of that.

You may begin to recognize in which relationships you feel fully seen and wholly accepted, where you feel trust and loyalty. Now is an aligned time to "edit" your relationships. Time is the most precious gift we can give to anyone—and Scorpio knows deeply and intimately that darkness is around the corner. So live in the moment. Protect and defend your time and energy and use this season to foster deeper connections and relationships with those who value you. Being vulnerable can be incredibly uncomfortable, but like most things, it becomes easier with practice. Tune into your intuition and trust what it reveals about particular connections and relationships in your life—past and present.

As a fixed water sign, Scorpio also has a strong emotional connection to the past. We may get caught replaying old scenarios in love or feeling guilty or shameful about old dynamics and patterns If you're feeling heavy about old relationships, now is the time to embrace those feelings. Remind yourself of your growth and progress. Allow yourself to grieve Scorpio season can be a powerful time to transform the way you accept and give love. Choose to trust that a new beginning is possible. When you sit with your uncomfortable memories or feelings and work through them, you open the door to transformation. This new beginning offers a deepening of connections; whether you are single or coupled, you can form deeper bonds and step into connections that value intimacy and sharing truths with one another.

HOW TO MANIFEST DURING SCORPIO SEASON: SEX MAGICK 101

The power of an orgasm is not to be taken for granted. Scorpio season's manifestation hack is straightforward and involves getting intimate with yourself with a little sex magick. Scorpio is associated with the genitals, organs that can quite literally create life. And while sex is such a natural part of life, masturbation is often associated with shame, guilt, or fear—all feelings that Scorpio is intimately familiar with as it moves through the shadows and wades in the waters of the taboo. Spending time with your own body and appreciating its curves or angles and unique design is a beautiful and healthy way to channel your own raw and primal sexual essence for manifestation. Select a desire that you'd like to call in, then visualize yourself in a reality where you already have it. Focus on the details, noticing the people around you, how you speak, and what you're wearing.

As you build toward your climax, visualize those details of your desire again. Pairing your pleasure with your intention can change your life. As you get closer and closer to orgasm, and physical pleasure rushes through your being, associate those physical sensations with your manifestation. Trust that what you are experiencing in the physical now is confirmation that you have already achieved your desire in another realm. The Universe is conspiring to bring you your desire now. You've felt it—you have proof! After you finish, associate the rush of pleasure and buzzing throughout your body with gratitude.

TRY THIS!

If you feel safe enough to do so, share something taboo with your partner. Do you have any specific kinks or fantasies that you want to play out in the bedroom? Tap into Scorpio's raw and primal nature and be vulnerable with one another. Release judgment and, as long as you're both consenting, spice up your foreplay and try something new during sex.

SCORPIO SEASON **MOON MAGICK**

Each Scorpio season includes a new moon in Scorpio and a full moon in Taurus. The Taurus-Scorpio axis brings our attention to hope and promise for the future and the release of the past and what's no longer working. The days these lunations take place will vary slightly year to year. The following ideas can help you make the most of these windows of transformation.

New Moon in Scorpio

The new moon in Scorpio reminds us that new beginnings require the end of something else. While all new moons correspond with a fresh cycle, there can be a sense of loss, regret, shame, or sadness that looms in the air during this lunation. The moon, a planet that's associated with comfort and nurturing, doesn't exactly thrive in defensive and dark Scorpio. We may face our shadow or emotions that we've buried deep within. Our skeletons don't come out of our closet to punish but to encourage us to engage in the sacred act of purging. A new beginning is so close, but first we must release and remove parts of our past that are taking up too much of our mental or emotional energy.

The new moon in Scorpio is an aligned time to reconnect with your personal power. It's time to reclaim it. Psychologically minded, the new moon in Scorpio can also hold a mirror up to ourselves and show us the truth behind our motivations, fears, and desires and allow us to experience a newfound sense of alchemy as our inner and outer selves reconnect and understand one another on a deeper level. This is the time to release the past, forgive yourself and others, and surrender and trust the process. Engaging in healing work can be especially empowering at this time. Your intuition may also be heightened, so pay attention to symbols in your dreams or signs from your Spirit team. We are ready to dive into the unknown trusting wholeheartedly that the Universe will catch us and support us at just the right moment.

Full Moon in Taurus

Taurus and Scorpio connect us with our physical beings through sensuality, pleasure, fears, and our desires. Together, they make up the axis of life and death. The moon adores to move through hedonistic Taurus, where it feels comfortable to indulge in its sensual desires and habits. With the Sun sitting across the sky in complicated Scorpio, we are reminded to strike a balance between being lost in our complex emotions and enjoying the natural simplistic luxuries of life. The full moon in Taurus asks you, "Do you feel safe enough to be present?" This is an aligned time to engage in embodiment and somatic practices that remind you of your humanness and with the Sun in Scorpio, even your fragility.

Matters related to love, personal values, finances, and whatever seeds you planted during the new moon in Taurus at the beginning of the year may reach their climax. If you've been working tirelessly toward a goal, it may be time you've reached a milestone or accomplishment. And, with that, in true Scorpio fashion, a sense of bittersweetness bubbles to the surface. For Scorpio knows that it's not the desire that leads to fulfillment but the process and journey. Reaching the top can be a lonely place. As you reflect on the two signs that both give life and take it away, this full moon asks you to find appreciation and acceptance for both parts of the process.

Moon Water

Using the element of water, we can harness the power and magick of the moon's energy and lifeforce by making moon water. Moon water can be used to alchemize our fears, anxieties, shadows, and pain and turn them into a source of empowerment. Depending on what you choose to focus on, you can use moon water to remove energies from your life or bring a goal or manifestation to life.

- *Glass of water*
- *Clear quartz*
- *Paper*
- *Pencil*

1. Fill a glass of water, place a clean, clear quartz crystal inside of it, and place it, covered, either outside under the moonlight or on a windowsill overnight; somewhere it can soak up the moon's beams.

2. On a piece of paper with a pencil, write your petition or intention. Address it to the moon and asks for its help and assistance in either clearing out something you want to release or calling in a desired outcome in your life. For some extra cosmic assistance, do this when the moon is in Cancer, Scorpio, or Pisces.

3. If you are focusing on a manifestation, drink the moon water and visualize your intention as the water moves down and throughout your body. If you are hoping to remove something from your life, flush the water down the toilet and then burn your petition. You don't have to use the moon water the very next day; if you're using it in manifestation work, you can use it after a new moon, when the moon continues to gain light. If you're using it to release, use it after a full moon as the moon wanes.

SCORPIO
AFFIRMATIONS

My vulnerability sets me free.

I am not afraid of to dive deep.

Every part of me deserves to be loved.

I am bigger than my shame, guilt, and fear. I am a resilient being.

My focus and determination are unparalleled.

In times of doubt, I am reminded of my resilience.

I choose to learn from my fear.

My passionate nature inspires others.

I am proud to be profound.

I release the need to control.

My magnetism attracts aligned connections and opportunities.

My instinct and intuition are my guiding forces.

I am grateful for my pain and choose to learn from it.

Aim higher and dream bigger than you ever thought possible.

Seek answers in unknown places.

Enjoy the never-ending quest for knowledge, wisdom, and growth.

CHAPTER 9

SAGITTARIUS SEASON

November 22–December 22

There is a break in the storm—the dark and tempestuous rain clouds begin to clear, and a rainbow emerges in the distance. Sagittarius season arrives on the scene casually late with party streamers in hand. Finally, we get to feel the relief, promise, and hope we need after enduring a few dark nights of the soul during Scorpio season. Scorpio season gifted us many opportunities to learn lessons about our life path and what's been holding us back— now it's time to apply our newfound wisdom. Optimistic and seemingly carefree, Sagittarius energy is always up for an adventure and eager to live life to the fullest. When you've gone to hell and back again, it makes it a little easier to take a risk.

We arrive in Sagittarius season, feeling unshakable; our confidence has been restored. We've faced our demons, stared them down, and rather than running away, we decided to sit down and chat over a cup of tea. We've seen the darkness and we're reminded that there's nothing we can't handle. Aimed high toward the sky, Sagittarius is symbolized by the Archer, a centaur armed with a bow and arrow. Centaurs are mythical creatures–half human and half horse, which speaks to Sagittarius' mutable and ever-changing nature. This zodiac sign is wise and philosophical, but can also be extremely indulgent and lean into its beastial nature.

Sagittarius season is all about sharing, communicating, and learning. What do you stand for? Sagittarius is ruled by expansive Jupiter, the planet of wisdom, spirituality, and growth. Our minds are fertile for more knowledge, and the best way to learn is through experience (and some trial and error). It's time to take risks, explore uncharted territory, and check things off your bucket list. Travel—physical, mental, or spiritual—is also highlighted during Sagittarius season. You may find yourself ready to book an international vacation, take a psychedelic trip, or explore the meaning of life. As a mutable sign that thrives off versatility, Sagittarius loves to soak up new experiences and has wide-ranging interests and passions. As you try to experience as many things as possible, it may be difficult to choose—and focus on— just one at a time. The world is your oyster!

Sagittarius season also marks a transitional time in the zodiac; it's the last fire sign of the zodiac and the final zodiac season in fall before winter takes over the skies. If Aries season was the initial spark and Leo season focused on sustaining the fire, Sagittarius season incorporates our newfound wisdom so we can create something useful with the flames. With a fiery arrow aimed skyward, Sagittarius sees endless options without being confined by limitations. Their curiosity and positive mindset make them eager to soak up knowledge that can be applied in the season to come. The exchange of information is also a major focus—and we may find ourselves becoming more brutally honest with others and ourselves. Sagittarius season reminds us that luck follows when we take risks and take a leap of faith. With lucky Jupiter as its guiding planet, we may experience more blessings or become more aware and conscious of everything we have in our lives during this season. Gratitude becomes a daily practice and we remember that our future really is limitless, as long as we learn to appreciate the here and now and dare to dream big.

Take a Trip:	Sagittarius knows the benefit of letting their curiosity steer the ship. As a fire sign and a mutable sign that prefers variety, Sagittarius not only wants to learn new things but wants to do so by soaking up different cultures, traditions, and experiences. Long distance travel is a privilege, and if it isn't in your budget, do what you can to shake up your current routine. Try a different route on your commute to work. Take your dog on a walk in a new area. Plan a weekend getaway to a nearby town you've never explored. Disrupting your routine and inviting new experiences into your environment will awaken some inspiration from within.
Learn a New Skill:	Sagittarius is known for a thirst for knowledge. We're more inquisitive and more easily distracted; with our shortened attention spans, we need something new to grab our attention. Learning a new skill, whether it's a language, a dance style, a new craft, or an extreme sport, will keep the mind engaged and provide the dose of exhilaration we crave. Trying new things often brings up a fear of failure, but by pushing outside your comfort zone, you remember that your potential is limitless. And if you fall, you can get back up.
Gratitude List:	Sagittarius season brings an optimistic outlook. But before you get lost in imagining the promise of your future, be grateful for where you are now. Start your morning with a gratitude practice. It can be really simple: As you're showering or washing your face, name five things you're grateful for. End your night the same way. Focusing on blessings is a mood booster and a reminder of what's possible.

YOUR LOVE LIFE + SAGITTARIUS SEASON

Grab your go bag—adventure awaits! Love during Sagittarius season is spontaneous and lights our souls on fire. As the explorer of the zodiac, Sagittarius doesn't want to stay inside binge-watching your favorite show together. Sagittarius season reminds us that life is worth living and to the fullest! We're more apt to take risks, try new things, or go on romantic weekend getaways. Couples could benefit from proactively planning some dates that nudge each other out of their comfort zones. Sagittarius isn't a sign that knows how to do something half-heartedly—we're ready to go full throttle. Think skydiving, bungee jumping, cave diving, white water rafting, or scuba diving off the coast. We want to experience the extremes of the elements on Earth and share that life-altering experience together. With an increase of adrenaline, we feel more alive than ever and can appreciate our love for one another more. Singles may find a stroke of luck in the dating world by also putting themselves out there and trying new things.

As one of the most independent signs, Sagittarius reminds us that freedom and trust go hand in hand. If someone asks us to share our location with them, we might be more turned off than normal. It's not that we don't want to spend time with our partners, but we want to know there is trust established when we do go our separate ways and prioritize our individual hobbies and passions. There is rarely anything more of a buzzkill for Sagittarius than someone who craves control over what we do, who we see, and how we spend our time. Spending time away from our partners or, for singles, focusing on your own desires brings us more clarity in who we are. Sagittarius season awakens our sovereign nature.

When we do choose to spend our time with others, we want someone who will enrich our lives. Sagittarius is a sign incredibly wise beyond its years and has an insatiable thirst for learning. It can be beneficial to date someone who isn't our normal "type" during Sagittarius season. A simple definition of insanity is repeating the same thing over and over and expecting different results: So why not share your time with someone new? We want to learn from someone and even feel tested by someone who challenges our current perspective. Sagittarius knows there is wisdom in every growing pain.

HOW TO MANIFEST DURING SAGITTARIUS SEASON: MAKE A VISION BOARD

Sagittarius is an impatient sign, and when inspiration hits, they're ready to strike! One of the quickest ways to move faster toward your goals is to see it in front of you. With a little glue, a pair of scissors, and some intentional images, you can craft your future from your couch with a vision board. When we see the images, symbols, or words that encapsulate our goals or visions in front of us and in our presence, it makes it easier for us to feel into that timeline and possibility. A vision board can be a creative way to build a roadmap to your desired destination and manifestations.

Grab some craft paper, old magazines, and maybe even some glitter to call in the essence of abundance—piecing together your future in a visual sense will feel productive and help you expand your current dreams. There's no need to limit yourself; as you sift through images that feel resonant or representative of what you're calling in, you may feel inspired by other sights, too. It's all fair game. Trust your intuition when it comes to what you place on your vision board. There's no right or wrong way to do this.

TRY THIS!

If you struggle with releasing your manifestation, staring at what you want but don't have can feel maddening. Solution: Set a time limit with your vision board. Keep it up for a full lunar cycle and then, when you're ready, take it down from your wall. Consciously state that you trust the Universe to act in divine timing.

SAGITTARIUS SEASON **MOON MAGICK**

Each Sagittarius season includes a new moon in Sagittarius and a full moon in Gemini. The Gemini-Sagittarius axis focuses on the exchange of information and ideas. The days these lunations take place will vary slightly year to year. The following ideas can help you make the most of these windows of opportunity.

New Moon in Sagittarius

It's time to make a wish! The new moon in Sagittarius reignites our inner spark and courage to dream big. If you knew there were no limits to what you could achieve, what would you ask the Universe for? New moons mark the start of a new chapter, and in Sagittarius, we're feeling hopeful and optimistic about where the future is headed. Sagittarius loves to take a good risk—so this new moon dares you to shoot your shot and bet on yourself. It's time to zoom out and shift your perspective. Thinking big will increase your confidence. Sometimes taking a leap before you're ready is what brings the reward you've been dreaming of.

As a fire sign, Sagittarius also has bundles of momentum and energy behind it. Not simply manifesting and visualizing our future reality, we tap into our inner well of blind faith and take a bold step toward it with action. Knowledge, learning, and expanding our worldview are also key components of this new moon. Think about the ways in which your current perspective might be limiting and in what areas of your life you may be opting for the status quo. Overzealous Sagittarius demands adaptability and change. While that comfort zone has served a purpose, trying new things and daring to dream bigger than before will feel natural now. We're ready to aim our arrow toward the sky and curious to see how the Universe will surprise us and reward us for moving in an unfamiliar direction with a sense of faith and trust.

Full Moon in Gemini

It's time to speak our minds. The full moon in Gemini lights up the sky and encourages us to self-express. If you've been avoiding some hairy truths, you can't avoid them for much longer. This lunation reminds you that the truth sets you free. But first you must find the courage to use your words. With the sun and moon on the axis of information, you may learn something under this full moon that shifts your perspective or plans for how you'd like to move forward. Gemini reigns over the realm of duality—and you may be caught between two planes, wondering which to choose. But what if you don't have to choose? The full moon in Gemini asks us to examine the information we absorb and consider if we are actively applying that new knowledge in our daily lives.

Sharing your views, special skills, or feelings with others may feel like a compulsive, yet necessary, reaction under these moonbeams. Now is the time to share the knowledge you've gained over the past six months. Seeds and manifestations planted during the new moon in Gemini also may come to fruition. Alternatively, you may feel ready to release those goals in exchange for a new path.

Connecting with others in our community and sharing our light with our loved ones is also a divine use of this energy. Our curiosity guides us under this full moon, and we know that we can learn the most by spending time in other people's energy—especially those who challenge us in positive ways. Writing, journaling, singing, and even screaming are all powerful ways to kickstart your voice and awaken any truths that have been lying dormant within.

TRY THIS!

Make a list of your fears. Pick one fear off your list and develop a plan for how to conquer it. Usually it's the things that frighten us the most that are what will bring the most change when we risk failure and choose to embrace the unknown.

Planetary Prayer

We're going old school, back into ancient times for this Sagittarius season ritual. We'll be crafting a planetary prayer to Jupiter, Sagittarius' guiding planet and the planet of luck, wisdom, and expansion. Many ancient astrologers associated Sagittarius with diviners, oracles, astrologers, and those who practice magick. So it only makes sense we try out some astrological magick during Sagittarius season.

We'll be crafting a planetary petition or prayer to Jupiter, asking the planet of expansion to bless us with our desires and, in exchange, we will honor its presence in our lives and send gratitude for the gifts it has brought our way.

Every planet has a day of the week it's associated with; these are known as planetary days. For Jupiter, that day is Thursday, so you'll want to make sure to plan this ritual for a Thursday for it to be the most effective. Set some time aside either first thing in the morning as the Sun rises or around midday; that's when we'll be petitioning Jupiter.

- *Piece of paper*
- *Pencil*
- *3 tea light candles (blue for extra credit, as it's the color associated with Jupiter)*
- *Amber incense*

(continued on page 108)

(continued from page 107)

1. Write a prayer or petition on a piece of paper. Something you hope to manifest. Address it to Jupiter like you would in a letter and humbly ask for the planet's assistance in bringing your manifestations Earth-side.

2. Once your prayer is written, it's time to set the scene. Calling on the energy and wisdom of the planets isn't something to take lightly. Did you take a shower today? Is your ritual space clean? Act like you're getting ready for a first date—you're about to make a first impression with a planetary giant! Asking for this celestial giant's support should also include an offering. That's where the candles and incense come in.

3. Light the candles and incense as an offering to Jupiter. Recite your petition out loud and clearly ask for assistance in bringing your desire to life. Before you end the ritual, thank Jupiter for hearing your petition and all the blessings it has granted in your life thus far.

4. Repeat every Thursday and show up consistently. You should not open this portal if you are not willing to commit. If you wish to stop this practice, make sure you do a closing ritual and let Jupiter know. Thank Jupiter for its assistance.

SAGITTARIUS
AFFIRMATIONS

I am limitless.

I use my voice to speak up for those who need it most.

I am a forever student of the Universe.

My knowledge increases every day.

My optimistic outlook guides me to new miracles in my life.

My honesty opens doors.

Every risk I take leads me closer to the life of my dreams.

Life is a game and I choose to have fun.

I'm grateful for where I am and who I am.

My future is full of promise.

I deserve to dream bigger than I ever imagined.

My humor is a gift to others and to myself.

My intuition is my internal compass.

Time is precious—make the most of it.

Be appreciative of where you are now
instead of focusing on where you're headed.

Set boundaries as a sport.

CHAPTER 10

CAPRICORN SEASON

December 21–January 20

Bundle up! Capricorn season is here and it's time to warm up by putting in the work. Sagittarius season allowed us to dream big and to zoom out to examine the larger picture. While we may be full of inspiration and excitement about what the future holds, Capricorn season, which takes place between December 21 and January 20, is here to help us take practical action toward making those dreams a reality. The start of Capricorn season coincides with the Winter Solstice in the Northern Hemisphere, the shortest day of the year. Yule, a pagan tradition, marks the longest night of the year and the eventual return of the Sun. But before we can enjoy the Sun's increase of light and the bounty that comes with it, we must first embrace and exist within the darkness.

The Winter Solstice is both a marker of time and a moment when the veil between worlds is thin. Death and loss are often associated with winter, and during the longest night of the year, we feel the presence of the spirit realm. Capricorn season marks a significant turning point—ruled by Saturn, the planet of limits and time, we are starkly aware of our own resources, as well our relationship with time itself.

As we move through the season of the Sea-Goat (Capricorn's symbol, a mythical creature who can traverse through the harshest environments of both land and sea), our ambitious nature is reignited. What are we hoping to build in this world, and ultimately what legacy do we hope to leave behind? As we contemplate these life-altering questions, we naturally begin to ponder how we use our time and energy. Saturn is the lord of time, and Capricorn season reminds us that giving our time and energy toward someone or a particular project or cause is the greatest gift we can give. This is a powerful time to reflect on how you spend your time. It's the season to renegotiate our timing contracts with the world around us and find more efficient uses of our most precious resource.

As the final earth sign, Capricorn wants to create lasting structures in our lives that can withstand the test of time. We planted seeds during Taurus season, harvested our crops and refined our process during Virgo season, and now we establish our legacy. As a cardinal sign, Capricorn's enterprising energy lends them the drive and determination to climb to the top. Achievement, status, and recognition are often associated with this zodiac sign, and during Capricorn season we may be more aware of our own reputation or other's opinions and expectations of us. This is an aligned season to set boundaries and renegotiate your relationships; notice who is cheering for you when you finally reach the top and who seems to disappear.

With a strong desire to achieve in the air and a swell of practical, productive energy moving us toward our ambitions, this is also a good opportunity to reckon with our limits. Self-criticism can pop up during Capricorn season, and it's easy to get caught up in a loop of self-blaming or self-shaming. Practicing self-awareness and self-compassion is key for reaching new heights of achievement.

As we begin to see our labor finally bearing fruit, it's important to consciously choose to be present and to acknowledge what we have achieved. It's easy to get swept away and become concerned about our next milestone—Capricorn's relationship with time can easily anchor us in the past or future. But there is much wisdom and expansion in the ability to make space for joy and living in the moment. If we can't prioritize pleasure, celebrating our accomplishments, and where we are now, what's the point of working so hard anyways? Capricorn season reminds us that the motto "work hard, play hard" is symbiotic and the key to manifesting your dream life.

SELF-CARE TIPS FOR CAPRICORN SEASON

Grounding Practice:	Connect with the element of earth. Go outside and plant your hands and feet firmly on the ground. Visualize an energetic cord in the center of your palms and the bottoms of your feet extending into the center of the Earth. Imagine the cords pulsing with Earth's renewable source of energy. Acknowledge the sensations of the ground against your skin. This practice can help bring you back into your body to adopt a more present state of mind.
Letter to Your Future Self:	Capricorn season can bring out our inner planner and have us future-tripping. Rather than wondering what will be, take your power back by defining what your future plans are. Write a letter to your future self: What lessons are you grateful that you've learned and moved through? What skills or routines do you have now that you know will lead to your inevitable success? Clearly state your desires for the future and thank the future version of you for never giving up. Trust that you have the focus to experience this reality someday. Express gratitude for your future self and for the upcoming lessons, learnings, and experiences that will get you where you want to be.
Take Breaks:	With so much emphasis on productivity in our culture, it's hard to slow down without immediately feeling a sense of guilt or shame. Capricorn season doesn't exactly help with this. Capricorn's relationship with time can leave us feeling like we're racing against the clock. However, taking breaks and resting is actually productive! Allowing our bodies, spirits, and souls to rest is restorative, inspiring, and recentering. It's through the pauses that we're able to reflect and reassess, as well as engage in other activities that may inspire us in a new way. Resist the urge to push forward, tune into what your body is asking of you, and don't feel guilty hitting snooze on your alarm if your body is asking for a little reprieve.

YOUR LOVE LIFE + CAPRICORN SEASON

Here comes the reality check you've been avoiding—Capricorn season asks us to take love seriously. Our time is precious and if we choose to invest it in another person… well, they simply must be worth it. Let's be real—we're busy and we have dreams to accomplish! For singles, they may be moving through the dating world with a more discerning eye. Can you envision a future with this person or people? It's not that casual encounters and flings are completely off the table, but we're more cognizant of mutual investment in one another. We're ready to leave flaky behavior and situationships in the past. There is a maturing when it comes to matters of our hearts, whether we are ready to share that commitment with someone else or not. Capricorn season is the time to reflect on your relationship with stability, security, and safety. Think about the types of relationship dynamics and traits in someone else that would leave you feeling cared for and nourished. We're more apt to focus on what building a joint future looks like. During this season, you may have more serious discussions about the future or setting healthy boundaries within your relationship dynamics.

Action and effort matter more in this season because Capricorn knows that love is earned. Always a little guarded, there is a hesitancy toward just letting our emotional walls down. Building trust in a slow and consistent way is what makes our hearts open. We want to see proof that someone's actions match their words and intention. Now is the time to practice what you preach and put your intentions to the test.

Capricorn season may also see us protecting our hearts a little more. With Saturn as its guiding planet, Capricorn knows that all good things take time. What's the rush? We may be more turned off by those who try to pressure us to adapt our timelines or bend our boundaries. Capricorn season reminds us that no is a complete sentence and that our time, our energy, and all that we have achieved is worth protecting.

HOW TO MANIFEST DURING CAPRICORN SEASON: PHYSICAL OBJECTS + DAILY GRATITUDE

As an earth sign, Capricorn likes to keep it simple. Capricorn season's manifestation magick involves finding, purchasing, or creating a physical representation of what you are calling in. For example, if you want to win an Oscar, buy yourself a faux trophy statue online. Take it to a local shop and get it engraved with your name and maybe Oscars 2045—something that represents a timeline in the future of when you will achieve this goal. Having something tangible that you can experience right now will help you connect your future desire with your current reality and experience.

Another important practice to cultivate during Capricorn season is a daily gratitude practice. When we're obsessed with our timeline and "in the grind," we can put too much emphasis on what we don't have and what we lack. This creates a lack mindset that is counterproductive. When we focus on what we don't have, the Universe isn't able to meet us halfway. The vibration we are emitting is scarcity and so in return, the Universe recognizes that energy as our desire. This can be a self-fulfilling cyclical process until we shift our mind to focus on the ways that we experience abundance in the now. Scatter gratitude throughout your day, such as before you eat. Also take time to be thankful for the opportunity to release what is no longer serving you. Consider making a mental list as you take out the trash. However or whenever you do it, weaving gratitude into your daily life can draw more abundance into your life.

TRY THIS!

Have the difficult conversation regarding expectations and, if necessary, set some boundaries. If you've been avoiding a topic or feeling resentful in a relationship, remember that you deserve to honor and express your truth. Those who are meant to be in your life will understand and respect you for speaking up.

CAPRICORN SEASON **MOON MAGICK**

)) ◗ ● ● ● ◖ ((

Each Capricorn season includes a new moon in Capricorn and a full moon in Cancer. The Cancer-Capricorn axis brings our attention to the past and the future. The days these lunations take place shift each year. The following ideas can help you make the most of these portals.

New Moon in Capricorn

Where do you want to be six months from now? The new moon in Capricorn is the perfect time to set an intention around a goal, project, or ambition you hope to achieve in the tangible world. As a cardinal sign, Capricorn is all about initiating and taking action. Use this motivating energy to not only visualize your end goal but take one practical step to arrive there. For example, if you want to start a new business online, purchase a domain for your website or start playing around with logo ideas. The key to harnessing this lunation's energy is to just push forward even if you don't know how you'll get to your end result.

This is also a powerful time to do a boundary check. If you've slipped back into people-pleasing habits, this moon will remind you that you don't have access to unlimited time. Your time is valuable and if you're wasting it on people who take advantage of you or relationships that aren't reciprocal, now is a great opportunity to set boundaries as needed. When you say no to people or opportunities that don't feel aligned, the Universe recognizes that you now have space to be filled—and sends along a more aligned opportunity or connection.

This moon can also have us reflecting on our legacy and reputation. Spend some time reflecting on your 10-year plan, 20-year plan, and 30-year plan: Where do you want to be, and who do you want to be? Don't be afraid to dream big and trust that with consistency, focus, and determination you will get there.

Full Moon in Cancer

A big release is on the horizon when the full moon in Cancer lights up the sky. Coming through in a sensitive water sign, the Cancer full moon invites us to reflect on our relationships with security and comfort—which can be a sensitive topic! Relationships of all sorts—family, romantic, platonic, or work-related—are up for review under these moonbeams. Do we feel cared for and protected by those we work so hard to protect? Now is also the time to prioritize comfort; release your fear of missing out. If you want to stay in and binge Netflix, why not? We're also asked to reflect on the generational patterns that exist within our family line and ancestry. Think about the habits and patterns in your biological or chosen family and how they might unconsciously manifest in your own actions. You may start to recognize how your family's expectations influence what you once aimed to achieve in the world. If your goals cater to others' wishes for you and your life, it may be time to make a change. Discussions or changes within family dynamics and living situations can also take place, as well as the realization that you may crave more privacy.

Nostalgic Cancer also brings up the past. Now is a profound time to release old stories, habits, or memories that keep you playing small. Forgiveness is a big theme, whether you're forgiving others or yourself. Sorting through old memories isn't for the faint of heart and can lead to big feelings. The full moon in Cancer asks us to be present with our emotions and make space for them. Our emotions are valid, and we deserve to mourn. If you're not sorting through emotional turmoil, the Cancer full moon can also encourage sentimental expressions and speaking from the heart. Don't be afraid to share how you really feel. The truth will set you free.

Personal Timeline Rewind

Focused on the future and long-term goals, Capricorn tends to gloss over celebrating all they've accomplished to reach this point in their life. To charge ahead toward what we hope to achieve, we must first be grateful for where we are now and how we got here. It's time to get a little retrospective with a magick-infused timeline that honors and revisits your past, highlighting what led you to this point in your life and spending a little dedicated time with your wins. Feeling into this state of gratitude for how far you've come, will bring you closer to where you hope to go.

- *Construction paper*
- *Colored markers*
- *Glitter*

1. Draw a timeline that starts with the year you were born at one end and the current year at the other end.

2. Mark important dates, setbacks, lessons, achievements and losses from your life along the timeline. Use color and glitter to represent the energy of that time period in your life and the impact that particular event had on who you are today.

3. No matter what the event, see if you can find some silver lining or lesson that helped you grow and evolve. In your journal, write a gratitude statement for each event on your timeline. Repeat these out loud once a week during Capricorn season and end with, "I am so grateful for who I was and who I've become and am so incredibly proud of myself for who I'm becoming."

You
Are
Here

CAPRICORN
AFFIRMATIONS

I choose to protect and honor my time.

My boundaries are deserving of respect.

I trust my dreams will come true.

When I invite more play into my life, I am more successful.

I trust my discipline will lead me to where I want to be.

My time is the most precious gift I can give.

I am grateful for where I am now.

I am well-equipped to handle any situation.

I trust I am meant for great things.

Honoring my rest is more productive than pushing forward.

Time is a construct; I am always in alignment.

It is safe for me to feel my feelings.

Leave your comfort zone in the dust.

Consider the collective and leave the world better than you found it.

Make space for innovative ideas to arrive.

CHAPTER 11

AQUARIUS SEASON

January 21–February 17

It's time to shake off the status quo—Aquarius season nudges us out of our comfort zone! We climbed our way to the top during Capricorn season, using focus and dedication to slowly, consistently reach our goals. But Aquarius season brings a realization: It's lonely at the top of the mountain. What is all of this effort worth if we don't have anyone to share our success with and celebrate? Achieving personal goals is great, but if we are going to leave a lasting legacy that truly matters, it's time to consider how we can impact others and the world around us. As the final air sign, Aquarius takes our thoughts and ideas and shapes them into something solid and lasting.

Aquarius is an air sign, but is often confused for a water sign because its symbolized by the Water Bearer, a figure pouring water onto the lands. In doing so, the Water Bearer nourishes the land and offers the collective a formative, life-sustaining resource. Aquarius is concerned with sharing its wisdom for the betterment of society and, ultimately, Earth.

Innovation, sudden insight, and breakthroughs permeate Aquarius season. We're considering solutions that might make us temporarily uncomfortable. As the humanitarian of the zodiac, Aquarius is concerned with progress. Also ruled by Saturn (like Capricorn), the planet of boundaries, time and limits, Aquarius is keenly aware of people on the fringes of society.

Aquarius' association with the archetype of the outsider is in part what lends to their eccentric, innovative, and individual nature. An earth sign, Capricorn's association with Saturn is expressed in the material realm—concerned with achievement, the material world, and the systems and structures that form the foundation of society. As an air sign, Aquarius' relationship to Saturn also focuses on systems and structures but places more emphasis on breaking new ground: creating ideas and intellectual systems that can impact the collective in the future.

Supremely social and inspired by interpersonal dynamics, Aquarius season reminds us to shift the focus from "me" to "we." How can we learn from our mistakes and outdated structures of the past to build a more sustainable and equitable future? Aquarius season awakens our inner rebel who knows that when we push against authority and societal expectations, new ideals that benefit the collective can be reached. It's always important to take time to reflect on your position and privilege in the world, but during Aquarius season you may find more courage to take meaningful action toward creating a world that benefits not only people like you but all people. Getting involved in an organization or volunteering for causes you believe in is a great use of this energy.

This is the season to push back on societal boundaries and personal limitations. We can visualize the ideal, and with Aquarius' fixed and determined energy, we can put an innovative plan in place to get there. During Aquarius season we may also approach matters from a detached perspective. We're less likely to let our emotions get the best of us but rather spend our time investigating our triggers with logic. Placing distance between us and our reactivity allows us to process challenging situations and feelings in a helpful way, lending clearer insight, and possibly leading to personal and emotional breakthroughs (just in time for Pisces season!). We're craving novelty and know that when we invest our time and care in community, everyone wins. Aquarius season reminds us that we are all human and, together, we create the fabric of society. It's time to be the change you wish to see in the world, even when it's not comfortable.

SELF-CARE TIPS FOR AQUARIUS SEASON

Journal:
As an air sign season, our mental faculties are busier than ever during Aquarius. Aquarius is often said to be aloof and detached from their emotional landscape, but they're not above overthinking. Journaling and using the written word are powerful tools to process our emotions and recognize which feelings matter and hold truth and which stories or things we tell ourselves from the past we are ready to release.

Build Community:
Aquarius yearns for change and progress and wants to see this shift reflected on a macro level. It knows the key to the expression: power in numbers. Spending time in other people's energy who share similar values can be both inspiring and recharging for the soul. Humans live in community for a reason! Cultivating your own community where you feel like your voice is heard and you feel like you belong can support your mental, physical, and spiritual health on so many levels.

Social Media Detox:
Associated with progress and innovation, Aquarius is also connected to technology. As social media platforms continue to emerge and gain more importance in our everyday lives, it has become easier and easier to get caught doomscrolling or waking up first thing and checking your phone. Practicing a conscious social media detox and choosing to be present in the world offers a powerful reframe. A social media detox can be a reminder of the value of true connections (as opposed to virtual relationships) and bring you back into your body. You'll have more gratitude for those who are a part of the daily fabric of your (real!) life.

YOUR LOVE LIFE + AQUARIUS SEASON

Welcome to sapiosexual season—love during Aquarius season reminds us that looks don't last forever, passion is fleeting, and intelligence can be the sexiest trait of all. As an air sign, Aquarius is concerned with the intellectual world. Partnering with someone (or multiple people) who can teach us something and enrich our minds feeds the soul. We want to not only feel seen but to be understood. There is a certain depth and bond that is formed when you know someone values the way you think and your opinions and can witness the beautiful and unique way your brain works. During Aquarius season, couples can reignite the bond by spending time doing crossword puzzles, starting a book club, attending trivia nights, or engaging in meaningful work together with an organization within their community. This season brings an increased desire to take action and participate in the change that we wish to see in the world. Sharing that progress and activity with your loved ones can make your connections feel more meaningful and fulfilling.

Aquarius season also reminds us that connecting with community and spending time in our trusted social groups nurtures our own relationship. From double dates to group outings to concerts, Aquarius season romance doesn't simply involve those in a relationship. Our curiosity is piqued, and we want to absorb as many new experiences as possible. Now is the time to plan that date night that always seemed like too much after a long day of work. Get a group together and go to an escape room. Tap into your inner child and plan a laser tag date. We want variety and to explore life—partly to tap into the too-cool-for-school Aquarius energy that can easily say, "Oh, yeah, I've done that," but also to shake up our tired routine. Boredom can lurk behind the scenes during Aquarius season, and if we find ourselves in a rut, that's our cue to try something new.

As an innovative and forward-thinking sign, Aquarius' association with technology can mean there's some extra luck in the air for singles while swiping on dating apps. Aquarius energy loves boundaries, loves knowing what to expect, and also loves that they have access to a new pool of potential lovers at the tip of their fingertips. Freedom is another major theme of Aquarius season. For couples, you may be addressing issues of co-dependency and learning to respect one another's need for some space. Smothering won't go over well, and there has to be a basic level of trust in one another to continue to build a sustainable union. If you're feeling distant from your partner, this may be a time to set expectations and boundaries around the time you spend together. Make a plan for which days you will spend together and set aside allotted time for you to pursue your own interests.

HOW TO MANIFEST DURING AQUARIUS SEASON: HIGH-DEF VISUALIZATION

Aquarius season is time for a daily visualization practice to get granular and detailed in projecting into our future timeline. Who is there with us? What do we look like? How do we act differently? What choices and habits are we making that differ from the current version of ourselves? When we can see it in our minds, it promotes a knowing that somewhere in the boundless vacuum that is space, other dimensions, and reality, it must be possible. We're choosing to remember that our dreams are implanted in our hearts and in our minds because they already exist somewhere, and our dreams are possible.

Another way to manifest your desires during Aquarius season is to try a guided hypnosis meditation. Aquarius is known for creative solutions and isn't above trying to reprogram their subconscious. You can search for a guided meditation video that aligns with your desire—like calling in more abundance or attracting more love into your life. If your desire is very specific, you can also set an intention before you engage in the self-hypnosis. Hypnosis has been said to increase relaxation, as well as improve focus and concentration. Reaching a more relaxed state, especially as we focus on our desires, can send powerful signals to the Universe and help magnetize our desires to us on a quicker timeline.

Warning: Hypnosis is best practiced in the evening before you go to bed. If you try this in the morning, you may be a little groggy throughout your day. Most importantly, don't attempt hypnosis while driving.

AQUARIUS SEASON **MOON MAGICK**

$)\ )\ \mathbf{)}\ \bullet\ \bullet\ \bullet\ \mathbf{(}\ (\ ($

Each Aquarius season includes a new moon in Aquarius and a full moon in Leo. The Leo-Aquarius axis brings our attention to the heart and the mind. The days these lunations take place shift each year. The following ideas can help you make the most of these portals.

New Moon in Aquarius

The new moon in Aquarius invites us to reflect on the structures we have in place in our life. Ruled by Saturn, the planet of time and reality, we may become more intimately aware of what's working and what's sustainable, and what we'd be better off without. This new moon can have both an innovative and exciting feel, as well as a sense of loss and moving on. Before we create new space for the world that we hope to build for ourselves (and the collective), we must release what isn't working and what is currently taking up space in our psyche. This lunation is perfect for setting boundaries in your relationships that will ultimately lead to a more inspiring life. Community is a big theme for Aquarius, and under these moonbeams you may also consider your relationship to your own communities. Where do you truly feel seen and appreciated and which of your social circles leave you feeling invisible and depleted?

We may also find an interest in reflecting on our own progress, dreams, and hopes for the future. This is a new moon that desires to awaken your biggest and boldest dreams and shake you free from your safety net. We become more aware of the bubble we've been existing within and can recognize that there's a reason we still are where we are—a fear of change! Aquarius' disruptive energy encourages us to step boldly out of our normal patterns to unite our actions with our ideas and dreams. Solution-oriented Aquarius will help us problem solve, as you make a plan to build what you truly desire. You may even find your ideas infused with brilliance.

Full Moon in Leo

You're centerstage with all spotlights on you—and that can feel a little vulnerable! The full moon in Leo asks us to roar proudly and share what's in our heart. Finding authentic alignment is fundamental under this lunation. Now is an aligned time to think about the path you are on and whether it is fulfilling. Remember, it's easy to blur the lines between personal fulfillment and making decisions based on the approval and expectations of others.

Now is the time to release any fears of taking up space and shout your message from the mountaintop. Self-expression and creativity are cornerstones of this lunation, and any personal projects or creative ventures started under the new moon in Leo during Leo season will reach their climax now. We're at a crossroads: Are we ready to move forward and take the next step, or is it time for us to step away and release an old goal? Leo often has a reputation for being self-centered, but it's actually a sign that struggles with being seen under its confident exterior. Now is the time to celebrate yourself for all you've accomplished and to please yourself rather than people-pleasing. Lean into your authenticity. There is no one else on Earth quite like you!

TRY THIS!

The full moon in Leo can also feel like a tender time. Perhaps you feel like you've teleported back to your childhood self. Spending time with your inner child or inner teen and doing guided meditations that send love, compassion, forgiveness, and care to the young version of yourself can be exceptionally healing at this time.

AQUARIUS SEASON RITUAL:
Gratitude in a Bottle

Surely, you've heard of messages in a bottle, but for Aquarius season's ritual we're doing gratitude in a bottle. This practice is simple, straightforward, and ongoing. We're going to track what we're grateful for and what manifestations come true throughout the year. This will get you in the practice of using the written word (Aquarius is an air sign, after all) on a regular basis to note your gratitude, acknowledge your wins, and encourage you to celebrate along the way. Cultivating gratefulness in our lives alters our energetic field in an expansive way.

- *Small pieces of paper (or sticky notes)*
- *Bottle, jar, or container of choice*
- *Decorative materials such as stickers, glitter, images or words from magazines, colorful paint or markers, ribbon, etc.*
- *Pen*

1. Once you choose a container, decorate it. You're going to be using it all year, so you'll want to make sure that when you look at it, it evokes all the warm feelings.

2. Write 10 things you're grateful for on 10 small pieces of paper. Place them in the container.

3. As you move through Aquarius season and the rest of the year, every time a manifestation comes true, write it down and put it in your magickal container. This exercise serves two purposes: At the end of the year, you can look back on all the magick you've made, and as you move through the year, if you need a pick-me-up, you can go re-read the messages you've written.

AQUARIUS
AFFIRMATIONS

My differences make the world a better place.

I choose to leave my comfort zone behind me.

I tend to the fertile soils of my mind regularly.

I choose to nurture connections that make me feel like I belong.

Teamwork makes the dream work.

I use my voice to speak up for injustice.

Investing in my community is investing in myself.

I hold space for my inner rebel.

Innovative ideas wash over me every day.

My thoughts don't define me.

Setting boundaries is second nature.

I choose to leave the world better than I found it.

Surrender to the unknown.

Lead with compassion and forgiveness.

Supercharge your relationship with the supernatural.

CHAPTER 12

PISCES SEASON

February 18–March 20

Life is about to get a little more emotional. As February draws to a close, we ditch the detached perspective of Aquarius season and embrace every feeling that life has to offer us in Pisces season. We've been busy prioritizing a logical and detached perspective so we can dream up solutions for a future world that celebrates progress and equity. Pisces season reminds us that despite the differences we celebrated in Aquarius, we are interconnected beings. Pisces is symbolized by two fish swimming in different directions. Pisces is an incredibly fluid and changeable sign. As the last zodiac sign, Pisces has an intimate relationship with the collective unconscious and other realms. The fish represent Pisces' daily challenge of sorting through fantasy versus reality.

Pisces season takes over the sky from roughly February 18 until March 20, and asks us to surrender, trust, and merge. As we reach the final zodiac sign and finish our journey around the zodiac wheel, we can step back and witness our growth and evolution. Pisces absorbs all of the lessons from the previous zodiac seasons—all the wins, setbacks, confrontations, pleasures, hopes, and fears. Pisces' compassion is unparalleled and one of the greatest gifts it offers us as we conclude our journey around the zodiac wheel. We are so much wiser for all we've been through. That wisdom is inherently tied to Pisces energy. For Pisces knows that we must feel, trust, and witness the humanity in all of us to truly thrive. It's here that we surrender our logical selves in favor of honoring the interconnectedness we all share as living, breathing beings on Earth. We return to source–and, soon, we will begin the cycle all over once again.

Ruled by Jupiter, the planet of spirituality and wisdom, Pisces season invites us to engage with the big emotions and feelings that we've been avoiding. As the final water sign, there is an understanding that tuning into our feelings and sharing them has the potential to set us free. As a mutable sign, Pisces also knows the complexity that exists around universal truths. It can see both sides to many issues, which helps us extend compassion and forgiveness to those who deserve it, including ourselves. There is, of course, a mystical quality that weaves throughout Pisces season; watching the rain beat against our windows or the sun rise and set feels like a spiritual practice. Our intuition is heightened. It can feel like the Universe is speaking to us in various ways. Pay attention to synchronicities, signs, and symbols in your dreams and waking life; the Universe and your Spirit team have you on speed dial during this transcendental season.

As we wrestle with the concept of surrender and trusting, Pisces season encourages us to have faith. What could we accomplish if we chose to leap into the unknown? Pisces knows life will continue to ebb, flow, entice, excite, and disappoint us—and that each wave in the flow of life is necessary. Pisces season reminds us that love is a universal language and we may feel some of our rough edges smooth out and our grudges dissolve. Now is the time to reconnect with your inner voice, be present with your emotions and, despite it all, choose to grieve and heal. Pisces knows that healing has no official finish line; it's part of the human experience and an ongoing process. And Pisces season reminds us that we can heal, dream big, suffer, mourn, and create the future we desire all simultaneously.

SELF-CARE TIPS FOR PISCES SEASON

Drink Lots of Water:
As we move through the emotional, ever-changing waters of Pisces season, it's critical to prepare our bodies for what's to come. Drinking water and nourishing our physical being reminds us that we are, in fact, human. It's easy to dissociate and get lost in fantasies during Pisces season. This simple, necessary daily practice reminds us that tending to our physical temple is just as important as tending to our spiritual self.

Say No:
Pisces energy can amplify the guilt associated with saying no or asserting our boundaries. You owe it to yourself to honor your boundaries and what will make you feel good. Saying no proactively and frequently helps this incredibly vital exercise become easier and easier each time. Your life won't shatter if you choose to say no, and those who love and respect you will respect your needs.

Psychic Self-Protection:
Deep-feeling Pisces knows no limits or boundaries. It's easy to feel into other people's experiences and emotions and take them on as our own. Engaging in daily psychic self-protection is key for clearing out unwanted energy and reconnecting with our own life force. Here are two simple ways to do so: When you wake up, visualize a reflective orb around you; anyone else's energy or words simply bounce off. Or, while you shower, as you scrub the suds along your body, imagine the dirt and grime that's washing off you as other people's energy that you're ready to release. As the soap swirls down the drain, trust that it is gone and that you are in your own energy once again.

YOUR LOVE LIFE + PISCES SEASON

Love during Pisces season is like diving into the depths of the sea. Traversing the unknown, we let down all our barriers and boundaries in exchange for merging our soul with another. Vulnerability and intimacy are threads that may work their way into our love lives during Pisces season. Romance is in the air, and there is a desire to enjoy all that life has to offer—with one another.

For singles, Pisces season may be a productive time to break down some of the walls you've built around yourself. It's an aligned time to reflect on the ways that you engage in self-sabotage when it comes to trusting and connecting with others romantically. We lead with our heart rather than our head at this time, and it's a powerful moment to put yourself out there if you've been wanting to re-enter the dating world. Sharing what's in your heart is favored during this season, making it a time to extend forgiveness or to release ties to past relationships that left you wounded.

Couples may find that their conversations become more substantial. Perhaps you're sharing memories you've buried deep within that have remained dormant for years. It's time to rebuild and reinforce trust in our connections. Sharing your hopes and dreams for the future, your kinks and desires, and what you love most about one another will feed your soul.

In Pisces season, sex can feel like a spiritual act. We may be cuddlier or seek more attention from our loved ones. Don't be afraid to make your needs known! If issues come up, be aware: Pisces is known for being avoidant. After all, the Pisces symbol is two fish swimming in different directions! When conflict arises, Pisces prefers to imagine a series of more peaceful events. We may get caught up in romanticizing people or situations or using escapism to cope. Do your best to stay on alert for red flags.

Pisces is also known for struggling with boundaries, so be careful of merging so deeply into one another that you lose your sense of self. As one of the most creative and romantic signs, Pisces loves to fantasize and idealize. During this season, it's easy to wear rose-colored glasses. Practice healthy boundary setting proactively. Allow yourself to get caught up in—but not carried away by—the wonder, possibility, and hope of it all. If you find yourself with your head in the clouds, look to ground yourself again.

HOW TO MANIFEST DURING PISCES SEASON: CHARGED WATER

As the final water sign of the zodiac, we're going to lean into that element to boost our manifestation power. Our bodies are made up of 60 percent water, so why not fill them up with some intentions via charged water? Grab your water bottle or the glass of water you're drinking out of for the day and fill it up. Next, write out desires and manifestations on pieces of tape; they can be as simple or complex as you desire. You can focus on feelings or experiences you would like your future self to have, such as peace, clarity, being grounded, or even a restorative night's sleep. If you have a specific dream, such as becoming a TV show host, don't be ashamed to spell it out! Next, tape your desires on the outside of your water glass or bottle. Let the glass of water charge under the moonlight for one night—either on a windowsill that can receive the moon's beams or outside. (If you place your water outside, cover it so you're not drinking anything unexpected from the outside world.) The next day, drink the water, and as you consume your intentions, visualize a reality where you already have what you desire.

Pisces also knows that when we feel good, we attract more positive energy and vibrations. Of course, we live in a world with much suffering, where people come from various backgrounds and possess different privileges. We don't all share the luxury of focusing on feeling good all the time. Pisces season invites us to acknowledge our pain, name it, and move through it to choose joy, despite it all. When we choose to have faith and cultivate more pleasure in our lives, we deepen our emotional reserves, and the Universe witnesses our resilience. Engaging in activities that feed our creative spirit and light us up attracts more of those feelings and opportunities into our lives. It's then that we truly understand the dual nature of Pisces—living in harmony with heaven and hell and choosing life and joy regardless.

TRY THIS!

The best time for setting new intentions and manifestation is just after the new moon cycle takes place. Time this practice a few days after the new moon, and as the moon grows and gains light in the sky, it will feed your intention.

PISCES SEASON **MOON MAGICK**

Each Pisces season includes a new moon in Pisces and a full moon in Virgo. The Virgo-Pisces axis brings our attention to service and sacrifice. The days these lunations take place shift each year. The following ideas can help you make the most of these mystical moons.

New Moon in Pisces

As the new moon darkens the skies, a beginning is around the corner. In Pisces, the final sign of the zodiac, this can feel a little counterintuitive. Pisces' journey through the zodiac wheel asks us to reflect on all we've learned. Ruled by spiritual and wise Jupiter, we are ready to integrate all of the knowledge we've gained on our path. We are also more understanding of the fact that being in control is often an illusion. There are many things we can't control in life and, for the most part, we must choose hope as we embrace the unknown. Pisces knows that surrender is a game-changing approach to life. When we release our focus on our desired outcomes, we are open to surprises from the Universe—some beyond even our wildest dreams.

The new moon in Pisces is a perfect time to take action and consciously choose to release someone or something. As you release stagnant energetic ties, you create more space for blessings to enter your life. Themes of healing and closure can coincide with the new moon, as we recognize the universal truth that we will never be done "healing"—and that being fully healed is more of a marketing ploy than an actual possible reality. Our imperfections are what make us perfect and unique beings. Acceptance, growth, and spiritual evolution comes with this new moon, as does self-compassion and self-forgiveness. Our psychic self is more active at this time, and we may experience tingles, signs, and synchronicities within the Universe or in our dreams. Your Spirit team is eager to communicate with you, so don't be afraid to ask for a sign or some assistance. We remember that it's safe for us to accept all of ourselves and reconnect with our intuition. In doing so we are then able to set goals and dreams for the future that would shock past versions of ourselves. We can finally dare to dream big, as we choose to trust in divine timing once more.

Full Moon in Virgo

It's harvesting season! Whatever intentions we set around the new moon in Virgo are coming to fruition or we're recognizing that it's time to release those original desires and adjust our plan. Virgo knows the benefits of small changes. If you've been looking for an excuse to kick a bad habit, this lunation offers a chance to improve your daily routine for the better. Virgo reminds us that true, lasting change doesn't have to arrive with a massive wave of disruption. It can be slow, steady, and calculated. This is also an aligned time to check in on your plan and strategy: Is it working and sustainable? If you've been caught in workaholic behaviors, now is a divine time to set boundaries around your schedule and make your needs known.

Quick to sacrifice and engage in some martyrdom, Virgo often forgets that being of service to ourselves first is key to helping others. You've got to put on your own oxygen mask before you can help others! Now is a good time to check in and ask yourself, how you like to be cared for. In what ways are your needs being met and not being met? Ruled by Mercury, the full moon in Virgo can also coincide with the arrival of news, sharing important information, or feeling ready to self-express.

TRY THIS!

The written word is more powerful during this lunation. With a piece of paper, write a list of habits you're ready to release. Then burn it. Trust that as you burn the piece of paper and watch the words disappear before your eyes, you are breaking ties with any former habits you hope to release.

PISCES SEASON RITUAL:
Cord-Cutting Visualization

There is no better season than Pisces season to be extra protective of our energy. Our visualization skills receive a cosmic boost during Pisces season, so we'll use that momentum to engage in a cord-cutting visualization to remove energetic connections that no longer serve us. Here's how to proactively protect your energetic field and release toxic ties to strengthen your boundary-setting skills and regain some energy.

1. Set the mood: Play some serene music, lay down, and get comfortable. Visualize a person, place, or thing that you feel overly fixated on. Pick someone or something that you feel is holding you back in some way. If that energy wasn't in your field, you know you could thrive even more.

2. Imagine a cord connecting you and the person, place, or thing. What does the cord look like? Are there thorns on it? Is it a dark and dim color? Where does the cord connect to your body? For example, if the cord connects to you through your heart space, you might want to consider doing some heart chakra meditations for the next few weeks for some extra healing, cleansing, and protection.

3. Imagine the cord almost has a heartbeat and feel it pulsing between you and what you're ready to release. Gently send warm and bright light and compassion through the cord. As you do this, visualize the slow disintegration of the cord. Know that as the cord disappears, the connection is released.

4. Affirm: "I release this connection so that all affected can reach their highest intention and timeline, with love and gratitude for what I've learned and who I am choosing to become."

PISCES
AFFIRMATIONS

It is safe for me to set boundaries.

My heart is my compass.

Creativity and inspiration flows through my veins.

I choose to trust in the highest timeline possible.

I witness miracles each day.

Spending time in my own energy recharges me.

I trust my intuition.

I have access to other realms and divine downloads.

Love is the greatest gift I can give.

We are all connected.

I am grateful for every human experience—the sorrow and the joy.

My soul yearns to evolve and grow.

My Spirit team guides and protects me.

The Universe is full of infinite blessings headed my way.

My depth and vulnerability are my superpowers.

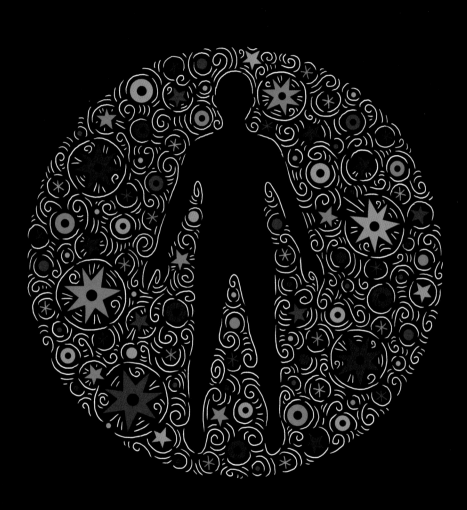

CHAPTER 13

COSMIC GRIMOIRE

There is no denying the magick that resides within each zodiac season. Once you have a solid understanding of what type of energy is available to you during each season, you can begin to layer additional practices to expand and enhance each season's magick. In this Cosmic Grimoire, you'll learn more about a few core principles that have forever transformed my personal practice, and I hope it will help strengthen your own magical practice, as well as the effectiveness of your spell work and rituals.

The ancient astrological concept of planetary days—each day of the week is associated with a specific planet and various meanings—packs a potent punch. For example, if you're hoping to launch a business or teach a course, aligning your launch day on Wednesday—Mercury's day, since Mercury is the planet of commerce and communication—can amplify the intentions of your venture and help you access the planets' energy.

Psychic self-defense is a necessary daily practice for any magical practitioner. Fortifying and protecting your own energetic field is key to practicing safely. Incorporating various herbs and spices into your spell work can also add protection or amplify your intentions. We'll also unpack the element of your zodiac sign to learn more about your manifestation style, and I've included some of my favorite Tarot spreads to use during the lunation cycle that aids in illuminating the next steps on your path. May your magical world continue to expand as you explore these practices.

PLANETARY DAYS + MAGICK

Each day of the week corresponds with one of the seven visible planets in the sky. Dating back thousands of years, astrological magicians (yes, magicians!) paid close attention to the time in which they chose to perform a ritual or do spellwork. When you align your intention with a window of time that is supported by the cosmos, it can amplify and make a spell more potent and powerful. For example, if you are doing a love spell or ritual, performing that on Friday would be ideal, as that's the day ruled by Venus, the planet of love, affection, and harmony. Of course, it's best to take in the entire astrology of the day before performing a particular ritual, but learning to use the planetary days as a baseline can weave some extra magick into your spellwork.

Monday	Moon
Tuesday	Mars
Wednesday	Mercury
Thursday	Jupiter
Friday	Venus
Saturday	Saturn
Sunday	Sun

Day	Planet	Suggested Uses
Monday	Moon	relationship with family; matters related to the home; comfort with change; growth; connecting with your body
Tuesday	Mars	taking action; calling in more courage; setting boundaries; releasing anger; strength and determination; confidence; protection
Wednesday	Mercury	improve reading and writing; support public speaking; clear communication; new ways to make money; successful business; obtaining knowledge; speaking your truth
Thursday	Jupiter	gaining wealth; gaining wisdom; improved health; seeking justice; good fortune and luck; improving spiritual practices and wisdom
Friday	Venus	connection with others; love; harmony; blessings with art and music; glamour magick
Saturday	Saturn	alleviating low vitality and depression; creating structure and commitment; processing grief or death; setting boundaries; releasing generational patterns/karma
Sunday	Sun	public recognition; physical vitality; authenticity; respect

TRY THIS!

For those of you who are ready to really dive into planetary magick, it also functions on an hourly basis. Every hour belongs to a different planet. Aligning your rituals with the corresponding planetary day and hour will pack a little extra of a cosmic punch. There are apps you can download that make it easy to track the planetary hours.

WITCHES' FAVORITE SPICES + HERBS FOR SPELLWORK

It's no secret that witches love herbs. The natural world is made up of so much magick that we often take for granted. Adding some of the natural world to our spellwork amplifies our intentions and increase. Here are some basic herbs you can use in your rituals and practice to boost your cosmic power and intentions.

rosemary	cleansing, purification, protection
cinnamon	grounding, abundance, protection, purifies a space
mint	money magick, healing, protection, psychic powers
bay leaf	dispels negative energy, offers protection
lavender	calming, increases psychic connection, releases anxiety, promotes rest
rose	love, self-love, growth, pleasure, joy, healing the heart

PSYCHIC SELF-DEFENSE 101:
HOW TO PROTECT YOURSELF BEFORE YOU CAST A SPELL

Before you do any spellwork, cleaning your space is essential. You want to perform your magick in a clean space so the energy is pure. This goes for you, too—did you shower that morning? Have you washed your hands recently? Before getting started, you want to be just as clean as your space so you're giving off the freshest vibes and clear energy. Especially if you're working with a deity—they're cosmic royalty! You wouldn't show up to meet your favorite rockstar without taking a shower, right? It's also important to cleanse your tools. For example, if you'll be using an athame, or dagger, to carve a sigil, or sign, into your candle, you can cleanse it with incense, clear quartz, tourmaline, moon water, or blessed water.

You'll also want to cast a circle before you begin any ritual work. To start, call on the elements, your ancestors, guides, or angels to assist, guide, and protect you. Visualize the perimeter of your circle and place your ritual items inside. If it feels aligned, place a candle at the North, West, South and East points of the circle. To cast a circle, close your eyes, focus on the North and repeat a statement of intention out loud. Here's an example: "I call on and petition the Spirits of the North to protect and bless me and this circle." State this for each direction of the circle, then trust you are safe and protected and you can begin your ritual work.

HOW TO MANIFEST BASED ON YOUR ZODIAC SIGN

This book includes manifestation tips for each zodiac season, but you can also manifest based on your zodiac sign. One way to do this is to focus on your sign's element and quality. For example, if you're a Leo, a fixed fire sign, you're probably passionate and eager for forward momentum. You may find manifesting a little easier when you're focused on a specific goal that you know you can commit to on a regular basis and even more so once you start to see tangible results. On the other hand, if you're a mutable water sign like Pisces, you may prefer more fluidity with your manifesting. Rather than focusing on a rigid schedule or one specific desire, you may find that inviting in spaciousness and allowing yourself to focus on what feels right in the moment are key.

Another option is to look at your entire birth chart and see which element comprises most of your chart. You may be a Libra, but perhaps most of your planets are in watery Scorpio; in that case, manifesting like a water sign might feel better for you. When we're feeling stuck, leaning into the elemental nature of our zodiac signs and birth charts can help bring us out of a manifestation rut.

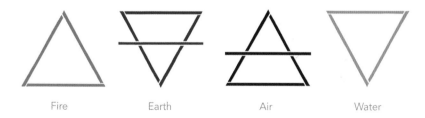

Fire   Earth   Air   Water

FIRE SIGNS
(Aries, Leo, Sagittarius)

This may sound counterintuitive, but the best way for fire signs to manifest is by letting go. Fire signs can be obsessively focused on moving forward and desire progress at all times. They're impulsive by nature and can be impatient. Fire signs can struggle with one of the key parts of the manifestation process: trust and surrender. To speed up your manifestation, rather than focusing your boundless energy on your desires, find an activity to do in the present that brings you joy. Find something that lights up your inner child and brings you back to the present moment. You're more likely to be surprised by the Universe when you're having fun and feeling grateful for the present.

EARTH SIGNS
(Taurus, Virgo, Capricorn)

Earth signs can speed up their manifestation processes by grounding back into their body. These zodiac signs are very concerned with the material realm and tangible results. They've got a process for everything and can get caught up focusing on planning the next step. This takes them away from the present moment. Reconnecting with their physical body and tuning into the present moment will help them stop focusing on what they don't have. Being present and living for the now is the secret to manifesting dreams beyond your wildest imagination.

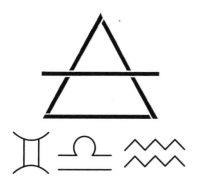

AIR SIGNS
(Gemini, Libra, Aquarius)

Speak your dreams into existence! Communicative air signs should focus on the spoken and written word. Talk about your hopes and visions for the future with a friend in vivid detail. Write a letter as your future self. Share your desires with others, no matter how outlandish they may be! We often feel resistance when it comes to sharing our dreams with others. Feelings of shame, embarrassment, or guilt can arise, thinking, Who am I to have the audacity to dream so big? Choosing to push through any discomfort and communicate about your desires, will weave your intention deeper into your subconscious mind. Bonus: Expressing what you want also sends clear signals to the Universe.

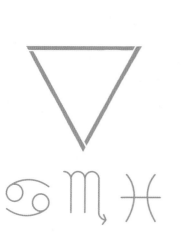

WATER SIGNS
(Cancer, Scorpio, Pisces)

Water signs should try manifesting by tapping deeper into their extensive emotional depths and feelings. Rather than simply visualizing your goals, feel into them with your body. Pretend that your desires have already come true. What do you feel like? Take on those emotions and know and trust that your desires are around the corner.

FULL MOON + NEW MOON TAROT SPREADS

New moons and full moons are perfect cosmic check-in points to reflect on your manifestation process. Using the depictions and symbols of tarot cards, coupled with your intuition, will offer you access to unseen realms and insight on your path forward.

The layout of the cards is the same whether you're reading under a full moon or a new moon; however, the positions of the cards have different meanings and respond to different questions. Use your intuition and adapt these questions as you see fit.

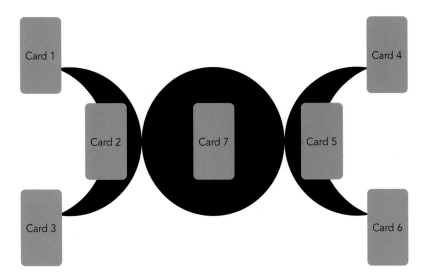

Full Moon Tarot Spread

Card 1:	What should I recognize and celebrate under this full moon?
Card 2:	What am I ready to let go of under this full moon?
Card 3:	What hidden truths are available to me now?
Card 4:	What advice does my Spirit team have for me during this lunar cycle?
Card 5:	What is my lesson during this lunar cycle?
Card 6:	What's the best way to support my desires under this lunar cycle?
Card 7:	What should I focus my energy on next?

New Moon Tarot Spread

Card 1:	What am I shedding and releasing?
Card 2:	What is emerging with this new moon?
Card 3:	What obstacles or challenges should I be aware of during this process?
Card 4:	What advice does my Spirit team have for me during this lunar cycle?
Card 5:	Which of my gifts should I focus on during this lunar cycle?
Card 6:	What type of support is available to me during this lunar cycle?
Card 7:	What is my immediate next step?

CONCLUSION

As we finish our tour around the zodiac wheel, I hope you leave feeling inspired and more in tune with the cosmic cycles that surround us. Astrology lends us the gift of awareness—and the opportunity to refine, reflect, and move through the world with a greater sense of compassion for ourselves and others, as well as a deeper understanding of the natural ebbs and flows in life. In a world conditioned on capitalistic principles, I hope moving through the zodiac and witnessing the seasons of expansion and contraction reminds you that rest is your right and a natural part of life. We aren't meant to go-go-go 24/7, and witnessing the cosmic cycles reminds us to extend ourselves the necessary grace, acceptance, and compassion.

As you continue to expand your spiritual and magical practices and hone your manifestation abilities, I encourage you to zoom out. How can you use this wisdom to help others and leave the world a better place than you found it? It's my hope that somewhere along the way, this book reminds you that we are all human—flawed, evolving, and forever transforming—perfectly imperfect creatures that are all interconnected. Caring for others is a sacred act and duty. Every creature and human on Earth deserve a sense of respect, peace, and love.

In your most mesmerizing and challenging times, I hope you're able to look to these cosmic cycles and seasons as mirrors of your own growth, eventual decay, and loss. To trust in the process and divine timing. Remember that you are worthy and deserving of any desire or wish that is planted in your heart. I hope you're reminded that it is a gift and miracle that you incarnated here at this moment—and for a reason. We are all made of carbon, oxygen, nitrogen, and phosphorus—elements that are released by stars into the vastness of space once a star dies. We are intertwined with the stars in this cosmic cycle and dance of life and death. Life is short, so be kind, leave the world better than you found it, take some risks, and most importantly, never forget that you are made of both starlight and magick.

ACKNOWLEDGMENTS

As a little Leo, I would daydream with my grandma about the day I'd write a book. As a Virgo moon, this is truly a dream come true. There are so many amazing humans and guiding forces in my life whose support offered me the encouragement, reassurance, and safety to believe in myself and bring this lifelong dream to fruition.

First, to my husband Joey, thank you for letting me use the excuse, "Don't you know I'm writing a book?!" for nearly everything for four consecutive months. Thank you for being my best friend. Thank you for making me laugh every single day. Thank you for feeding me—emotionally and, like, really cooking and feeding me. Thank you for holding me and wiping away my tears. Thank you for breathing inspiration and life back into me when I feel helpless, overwhelmed, or lost—and for always bringing me back to the present moment. I love you in every dimension and am forever your biggest fan.

To Sam Reynolds, thank you for bringing astrology to life. Thank you for sharing your wisdom in an engaging, informative, exciting, and enchanting way. Your classes and mentorship forever changed my practice as an astrologer, and your teachings made me understand astrology in a way I never thought possible. Erika Buenaflor, thank you for sharing your gifts and wisdom with me, and for your mentorship. Thank you for seeing me, for your encouragement, for your healing, and for helping me access a sacred space within myself and my own lineage.

Kaitlyn Graña, thank you for your gracious teachings and wisdom that reignited the connection and eternal flame between myself and the Spirit world. Gala Darling, thank you for sharing yourself and your experiences with EFT tapping to the world, and for your thoughtful and playful teachings and guidance on my journey to becoming a practitioner. Tapping with you made me fall in love with myself again and made me believe that all my desires and dreams are possible.

To my astrologer friends and colleagues, Maria, Laura, Lauren, Thea, and so many more, thank you for always sharing your love of the Cosmos with me. I learn and grow so much from each of you and our star-filled conversations. I am also so incredibly grateful for Annabel Gat's generous and welcoming teaching style and I've learned so much from her craft over the years. Julie Vader, thank you for your patience and mentorship as my first editor. I'm forever grateful and simply wouldn't be here without you. To my editor, Hilary—thank you for seeing something in me and believing in me. For your guidance and support throughout this entire process. Thank you for helping me birth and bring my dream to life.

To my biggest cheerleaders throughout this entire process (in alphabetical order!)–Amy-Lynn, Heather, Janet, Jen, Kate, Samantha, and Simone—thank you for your endless support and encouragement. For letting me ramble on about the stars every time I see you. I appreciate you all in every dimension. To my family— my sister, mom, dad, grandma, grandpa, all my uncles, and my aunts—thank you for always allowing me to be me, even if it doesn't make sense to you all the time. There are so many others to thank, but I can feel the Oscar music cueing up—from the bottom of my heart and soul, thank you to everyone for your support. I'm forever grateful in every dimension.

ABOUT THE AUTHOR

STEPHANIE CAMPOS is an astrologer, psychic medium, and witch. She's studied the mystical arts for over a decade including the stars, mediumship, palm reading, tarot, curanderismo, and more. She's passionate about being of service, helping others heal, and using astrology as a tool for transformation. Her work has also appeared in *Cosmopolitan*, Refinery29, *Well + Good*, and Bustle, among other publications, and she has appeared on the *Today* show as an astrology expert and modern mystic.

ABOUT THE ILLUSTRATOR

CAITLIN KEEGAN is a New York-based illustrator and the creator of The Illuminated Tarot and the Happy Houseplant series, published by Clarkson Potter. Caitlin loves bold color and detail and strives to create engaging work that is meaningful, intuitive, and inclusive. You can see more of her work at caitlinkeegan.com

INDEX